Sandwell
Metropolitan Borough Council

Please return this item to any Sandwell Library on or before the return date.

You may renew the item unless it has been reserved by another borrower.

You can renew your library items by using the 24/7 renewal hotline number - 0845 352 4949
or FREE online at opac-lib.sandwell.gov.uk

THANK YOU FOR USING YOUR LIBRARY

West

The
History

12623879

Front cover image courtesy of Robin Horton.

First published 2014

The History Press
The Mill, Brimscombe Port
Stroud, Gloucestershire, GL5 2QG
www.thehistorypress.co.uk

British Library Cataloguing in Publication Data.
A catalogue record for this book is available from the British Library.

ISBN 978 0 7509 6004 5

Typesetting and origination by The History Press
Printed in Malta by Gutenberg Press

Contents

Introduction

The West Midlands has made and continues to make a huge contribution to the story of the inland waterways of Great Britain. Yes the Birmingham Canal Navigations (BCN) has lost some of its original waterways, and that is a sad fact, but the BCN is still an amazing place to visit, and its history is rich and varied. Add that to the other great associated waterways – the Staffordshire and Worcestershire; the Worcester and Birmingham; the Trent and Mersey; and of course the River Severn, and you have enough waterways to spend a lifetime exploring.

Stourport is my first chapter of choice because, in 1772, that is where James Brindley placed the terminus of his Staffordshire and Worcestershire (S&W) Canal; and what a treasure that town has been for over 200 years. And, like many others, I have come to love its riverside promenade and activities, and of course its historic canal basins. Within the last few decades it has been a pleasure to watch the town and its basins develop from a truly rundown state in the 1960s, to a special position in the hearts of all waterways lovers today. There were no fancy holidays abroad for the average folks back in the 1960s; you went somewhere in the UK and liked it, and Stourport was where my family took me. And though we may not have the best weather in the world, the tables have turned somewhat, and many people from home and abroad are discovering what great locations for holidays this country has to offer.

Historical figures are an essential part of this book, and such noteworthies as Boulton and Watt, John Corbett and Josiah Wedgwood add to the tale of how the canals came to be and how useful they were to the eighteenth- and nineteenth-century industrialists and entrepreneurs. Of course contrasted with these worthies are the ordinary working boatmen, and I have been fortunate to be able to get the life stories of two to add to our understanding of the last few decades of the industrial canal. Sadly, I don't think that now, in the twenty-first century, there are many of them left to tell the tale.

At a horseboating demonstration at a recent boating rally, a young lady volunteer was heard to say, 'That doesn't look safe. I don't think the canals were designed for horses', prompting older ones to quickly put her right: that indeed the canals, and especially the towpath (there's a clue in the word) were designed for horses, just as much as they were made for narrowboats. So, I have included a short history of horseboating and how the Horseboating Society, and indeed the five small firms still operating horse-drawn boats for pleasure, are doing.

The story of the Droitwich Canal finishes our book off nicely, mainly because it is one of the real success stories of modern times, where two old canals have been amazingly restored to a high degree. Also, in recent years we have seen our waterways handed over from British Waterways (BW) to the new Canal Trust, so it will be interesting to see how things develop over the next decade or two. I have to say that I thought BW did a good job. Oh yes I know that they got a kicking from time to time from various sources, and it's probably a good thing for volunteer organisations to keep an eye on large governmental bodies, just to keep them in check. But one has to admire the professionalism of their technical staff, for example their hydrologist, Adam Comerford, and senior engineer on the Droitwich build, Jason Leach, are fine examples. So here's to the future.

Robert Davies, 2014

1

Stourport: Its History and Transformation

EARLY PLANS AND DEVELOPMENTS

The introduction of canals radically altered the transport system of the country, but they also played an important part in the distribution of the population. Where canals formed junctions, or made a connection with other forms of transport, new communities sprang up. Existing towns that received a canal also experienced a spurt of growth. In a handful of situations, such as that at Stourport, a whole new community became the result of the new transport interchange. By the middle half of the eighteenth century, the issue of transport was uppermost in the minds of West Midland merchants and industrialists. As far back as 1717 there had been a canal proposal by a Mr Congreve to connect the Severn with the Trent, and there was a later scheme by Sir Richard Whitworth. However, if that gentleman's connection had materialised, the route would have been much further to the north, completely missing out the growing industrial Black Country.

Certainly when I first arrived in Stourport as a child in 1966, this delightful Georgian town with its fascinating canal infrastructure was already a *fait accompli*, and I was blissfully unaware that 198 years previously (on Wednesday, 2 November 1768, to be precise) the noted engineer James Brindley had ridden his grey mare on to John Acton's stubble field, looking for a suitable location where he could join his Staffordshire and Worcestershire Canal to the River Severn. Initially he had planned to make a connection at the mouth of the Stour some few hundred yards away. Unfortunately, earlier in that same year, the confluence of the Stour and Severn had flooded badly, which made him change his mind, and he looked again at the 5 acre field owned by John Acton, the church warden at Lower Mitton.

Some time later, land was purchased, navvies turned up to do what navvies do best, and by 1771 the canal with its first basin (a wider section of canal for boats

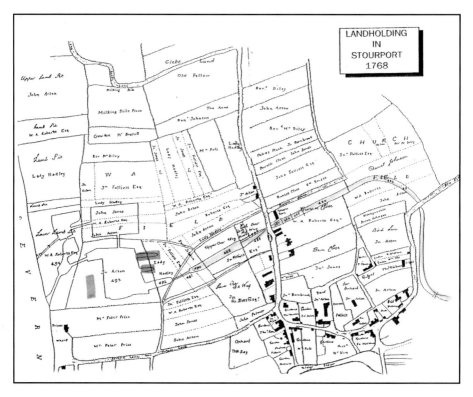

One of the earliest maps of the area showing the plots of land and who owned them. The canal can be seen entering Stourport from the east, going around the medieval Saxon village and entering the first basin. The later Clock Basin and narrow locks can also be seen.

to moor and unload) and initial set of barge locks was open for business. Then as the years went by, businesses of all kinds boomed and there came a natural need for more basins, warehouses and wharfing space. Stourport received the Clock Basin with its narrow locks in 1782, River Basin in 1805, and later the Lichfield Basin after 1806. (A later addition was the Cheapside Basin, which was connected to the Lichfield.)

STOURPORT BEFORE THE CANAL AGE

Simply put, until the Staffordshire and Worcestershire Canal arrived here in the last quarter of the eighteenth century, Stourport did not exist, though a small hamlet called Lower Mitton had stood since Saxon times some few hundred yards back from the Severn and near the River Stour. Traditionally, the scene around Lower Mitton had been one of rural tranquillity, while the busy coal and iron traffic of the Severn generally passed it by. Four miles upriver, the established town and port of Bewdley had for many years played an important part in the organisation of trade between the Midlands and the wider world due to the position of its bridge. Bewdley was a most important transhipment point, a focus of regular packhorse routes to and from Birmingham and other Midland towns.

Kidderminster, some 4 miles north-east of Stourport, and sited on the banks of the River Stour, had been a flourishing cloth-making centre since the middle of the seventeenth century, and though the Stour had been improved to transport coal between it and the more inland town of Stourbridge, the remaining 4 miles down to Stourport had remained in a poor state. Smaller rivers like the Stour had been historically important for the turning of water wheels rather than for transport routes. Some of the mills along the Stour were fulling mills, where fleeces were taken along for degreasing, the first step of the wool-making processes. However by the early 1770s, all of that was about to change. After the success of the Bridgwater

The earliest drawing of Stourport by James Sheriff (1776) though the mystery is how he actually gained this vantage point when there is no high ground directly across the bridge. The Tontine, stables and some warehouses are already in existence, as is the first river bridge, though not the narrow locks.

Canal, a Trent and Mersey Canal was promoted by Josiah Wedgwood with James Brindley as surveyor. Brindley envisioned the Trent and Mersey Canal as a main arterial route, with a Severn link coming from some point along this line. An Act of Parliament, created and approved for what was to become the Staffordshire and Worcestershire Canal, was short and vague and simply stated: 'An Act for making and maintaining a navigable Cut or Canal, from the River Severn, between Bewdley and Titton Brook, in the County of Worcester, to cross the Trent at or near Haywood Mill, in the County of Stafford, and to communicate with a Canal intended to be made between the said River and the River Mersey.'

So, the Act was pretty specific where the canal was to join the Trent and Mersey, but at the southern end there was about 6 miles of uncertainty. When Brindley made an early survey, and got as far as Kidderminster, which happened to be the last fixed point on the route, he was still imagining the Severn terminus at or near Bewdley. However, the Wolverhampton promoters had much influence on the matter and the final decision was to follow the valley of the Stour down to the confluence of the two rivers, and not go west over what would have been extremely difficult ground to Bewdley. This decision effectively became the two-edged sword that created the town of Stourport and caused the demise of the formerly flourishing town of Bewdley. Royal assent for the canal was given on the same date as that for the Trent and Mersey – 14 May 1766.

Of course the arrival of the canal at the mouth of the Stour was of great importance to the residents of Lower Mitton, and they watched with interest as engineers and navvies arrived to excavate and turn pasture land into basins and locks. Lower Mitton, the tiny hamlet, with a ferry some 400 yards downriver at

Aerial view across the freshly built council offices towards the basins and power station; late 1950s.

Stourport's second bridge built of iron and remarkably like the one further upriver at Ironbridge.

Red Rock, lay on the northern bank of the confluence of the Stour and Severn, and lay right across the route that the canal would have naturally taken, so the final line of the canal had to make a rather sharp 's' bend to go around the chapel and avoid the tiny medieval high street. The fledgling Staffordshire and Worcestershire Canal Company purchased a minimum of two fields to accommodate the first basin and dock, which were completed in 1771, though the traffic grew so rapidly that they quickly had to buy more land and excavate a second. An area was quickly set aside for the manufacture of bricks and tiles, and the first basin connected to the river via a small basin and two barge locks. From that time onward Stourport's growth and thus its future were firmly established.

Local newspapers like *Berrows Worcester Journal* ran regular advertisements for companies operating haulage services, especially when new canals and thus shorter routes proved profitable. Two advertisements in the *Hereford Journal* of March 1801 stated: 'The Thames and Severn Company putting on barges from Bristol and Stourport to London' and 'Boats leaving London for Stourport weekly, taking twenty-five days'.

A century before that and the Severn had been navigable as far as Pool Quay, way beyond Shrewsbury and almost as far as Welshpool. However, due to the work of draining the land around the upper reaches of the Severn valley for improvements in farming, the river's ability to take boating traffic had over the years seriously deteriorated. So in later years there were efforts to improve the river's channel and to make horse-towing paths along its banks, though it must be added that teams of men had been employed in bow-hauling river craft for the previous 200 years. In 1784, William Jessop was commissioned by the S&W to give an estimate for making improvements to the river. The company actually did some dredging between Stourport and Diglis, but ironically was taken to court for damaging the river. A later survey by Mylne, supported by funds of

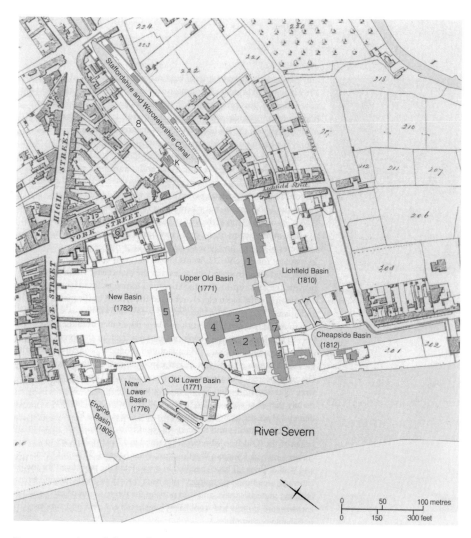

Stourport with its full complement of basins. 1. Long Room Warehouse; removed during the 1960s. 2. The Tontine. 3. Shed Warehouse; also removed during the middle of the twentieth century. 4. Iron Warehouse; later the lock keeper's office. 5. Clock Warehouse. 6. Aaron York's house, a successful early merchant. 7. Sail House, formerly Ames and Worthington's warehouse. 8. Canal Companies workshops (early twentieth century), later Canal Pleasurecraft boatyard and now new housing.

£10,000, gave impetus to further works, but these were so hated by river men that they vandalised any building activity done by the company.

The digging of the canal basin next to Lower Mitton started in 1768, and was in use three years later. The Staffordshire and Worcestershire Canal Company opened their head office in Wolverhampton, which was convenient amongst other considerations for being about halfway along the 46-mile canal. In 1774, only two years after the opening of the route, during what was probably the first pleasure trip along the Staffordshire and Worcestershire Canal, a young lady by the name of Elizabeth Prowse wrote in her journal, 'came to Storeport, a basson that covers three acres, with locks down into the Severen. Works done in five years by Mr Dadford, that is within 12 miles of Woster.'

With that brief entry, one can only conjure up an image of the freshness and vitality of that newly born enterprise. A local newspaper reported:

> This place is becoming the resort of people of fashion. The beauty of the country round about it, the fine navigable canal now completely finished, the spacious basin for the vessels, the River Severn, and the new bridge over it (brick abutments and cast iron centre designed by Thomas Pritchard of the Iron Bridge fame) form altogether a pleasing picture. Scarce a day passes but several parties of Ladies and Gentlemen come there in their carriages.

In 1893, 119 years later, the town was still attracting visitors, for *The Brierley Hill Advertiser*, on 13 May, delightfully wrote about Stourport's role as a pleasure resort. The opening paragraph stated:

The Tontine during the early part of the twenty-first century when it had ceased being operated as a public house and there were worries whether a new function would be found for this marvellous piece of canal heritage.

One of the early warehouses along Mart Lane – formerly Joynsons, now a chandler's.

This is an age of rushing to and fro [the reporter would swoon if he could be swiftly transported to the twentieth and twenty-first centuries]. The air is full of movement; the growth of education has led to an elevation in the tastes of the masses of the people. And, instead of spending their leisure hours in ill ventilated taverns, they get out into the green fields, and enjoy the beauties of nature, listen to the trill of the Lark and the song of the Linnet warbling through the vernal woods.

Fast forward to the start of the twenty-first century, and Stourport continues to attract the crowds to its plentiful amusements, though the lark and linnet have been sadly in decline.

Nevertheless the outcome could have been oh so different. At the time of the promotion of the Trent and Mersey Canal by Lord Gower, Josiah Wedgwood and others, another rival scheme under the leadership of Sir Richard Whitworth was also well under way. That plan was to take a canal east from the Severn just below Shrewsbury across to Stafford by way of Great Bridgeford. If this had been the successful contender, then the Staffordshire and Worcestershire Canal would never have been built, and thus Stourport would never have been what it is today. A slightly later scheme proved that Stourport's position as an inland port was as fragile and destructible as its first two river bridges, for in the 1790s the Dudley Canal Company, spearheaded by Lord Dudley, proposed an alternative canal, bypassing the lower half of the S&W, and thus Stourport. This parallel route would have gone from Stourbridge to Worcester by way of Bromsgrove. The bill for this particular canal was therefore bitterly opposed by the S&W, and was defeated when it went to the House of Lords. The S&W made sure that the bells of Stourport, Kidderminster and Wolverhampton were rung to celebrate this important triumph.

These are the great 'What ifs' of history. The Whitworth scheme, however, never really got off the drawing board, and a group of Wolverhampton businessmen headed by James Perry quickly promoted and surveyed the S&W that we know today, joining the Trent and Mersey at Great Haywood. Hugh Henshall and Samuel Simcock did an initial survey, and Brindley was employed for the final setting out of the line.

Stourport has therefore been one of Britain's premier inland waterway resorts for over 200 years. And, with recent maintenance programmes, coupled with the reinstatement of a historic bridge and canal basin – it has only improved. Back in the nineteenth century, the town's population stood at around 4,000, but its modern counterpart has risen to almost 20,000. For these modern inhabitants, Stourport is the place where they live, work and shop. But for the additional thousands of day-trippers who flock here every year from the Black Country conurbation, it's the place to have a picnic, take a ride on the fairground, promenade peacefully along the tree-lined river, and finish a very pleasant day out with fish and chips and a pint. For travelling narrowboat crews, who enter its vibrant collection of interlocking canal basins, it is possibly the most visually entertaining point on their itinerary.

The town of Stourport and its Georgian canal basins, where the Staffordshire and Worcestershire Canal connects with the River Severn, have been for some

Looking across the river towards the basins and Tontine in the early twentieth century. Many of the buildings including The Riverside Café have long gone. (Kidderminster Library)

years, one of the great attractions and focal points of a very popular cruising ring. Its creation, however, was just one of those wonderful historical happenstances – the Stourport Ring. This title alone is indicative of the town's status, because the ring also includes the City of Birmingham and the cathedral city of Worcester; but the title didn't go to either of those worthies. And so, each year, thousands of boaters choose to make their grand procession around this fascinating and very pleasurable route. As a consequence, traffic around the ring has grown steadily from the 1970s onward. In recent years, British Waterways have set counters at strategic points around the canal system to get a feel of boat movements. In 2009, 3,756 boats passed through York Street Lock, with 3,810 passing the same point one year later, giving a 1 per cent rise; statistics which will only get more interesting as the years pass by.

Private boat owners can of course enter the ring from all corners of the compass, while the majority of hire boaters tend to start their holiday on the Birmingham

Early twentieth-century view with Trows moored near the Angel. (Kidderminster Library)

and Worcester Canal as most of the hire bases are to be found on the southern half of this delightful rural canal. Years ago everyone seemed to travel clockwise; locking down to Worcester before heading upriver to Stourport, but more recently there seems to be a flow both ways. This popular, part rural, part urban ring has much to recommend it, containing such treasures as the Black Country Living Museum, the Severn Valley Railway and Sea Life Museum, to name just a few. For historical nuggets, one could list the Wast Hill and Netherton Tunnels, the birthplace of the Boulton and Watt Steam engine at Smethwick, and the glass cone and museum at Stourbridge. Yes, there is a wealth of interest around this circuit, and that's before you decide to spend a few days at Stourport itself.

As far as the town is concerned, there can be no doubt that it owes its very existence to the construction, development and prosperity of the S&W. The emphasis therefore is on its important junction with the arterial River Severn, and the bustling trade that operated within the canal basins and along the river frontage. Our early map shows the field layout of the eastern bank in 1768 (see page 8), just before development of the basins. The line of the canal has been set, and construction commenced. The first basin can be clearly seen, with its wide barge locks connecting it to the turbulent waters of the River Severn. The Severn had of course been a major trading route for hundreds of years, with an important transhipment point 4 miles upriver at Bewdley. The city of Worcester, an even more strategic trading place, is downriver some 14 miles away. Nevertheless, as navigation for large craft it had its drawbacks due to seasonal water shortages and shallow sections. This situation was vastly improved during the nineteenth century when extensive works were undertaken along the river to improve its depth.

As previously mentioned, it was the famous James Brindley who originally surveyed the line of the S&W, a survey paid for and promoted by a small group of Midlands entrepreneurs led by a Mr Perry. Brindley was, however, tied up with other pressing canal projects at the same time, and he tended to flit from one to the other, so the real day-to-day work was overseen by Thomas Dadford Senior, ably assisted by John Baker, Clerk of Works. The Act of Parliament that gave the go-ahead for the canal was passed in 1766, and the southern half from Wolverhampton to Stourport was completed four years later in 1770. Once this important section of the waterway was finished, the navvies were moved onto the northern half between Wolverhampton and its junction with the Trent and Mersey at Great Haywood. The whole canal, at just over 46 miles, was ready for through navigation in 1772.

NAMES AND BRIDGES

Names bandied about for the new port included Newport – not very original – and Stourmouth; but whatever this town was to be called, there was no stopping its speedy growth. There was no bridge over the river during those early years, and travellers wishing to cross to the opposite bank, had to go south along the lane about a thousand yards to the Redstone Ferry. On the west bank today you can still find the remains of some fascinating habitations cut into the sandstone cliff.

Over the last 200 years Stourport has had three bridges to grace its alluvial banks. The first received its approving Act in 1773. Work commenced in the following year, and it was ready for traffic the year after that. Travellers wishing to use it had to pay a toll. The first bridge, costing £8,000, was of mainly brick construction, with decorative stone facings. Altogether there were fifty-two arches that included the approaches and the three larger arches that spanned the actual river. Unfortunately, the life of this particular bridge was of short duration. The winter of 1794 was particularly severe across the Midlands and Wales, and the town's bridge, only twenty years old, had two of its river arches completely swept away during the winter's powerful torrents. And as the winter snows melted in the following spring, Bewdley's bridge met the same fate; as did Stamford Bridge on the River Teme. So, for the next ten years the locals and other traders had to make do with the ferry at Arley, another 4 miles upstream from Bewdley – not the finest arrangement. A second bridge opened in 1806, a year after the Battle of Trafalgar, but this time, the bridge trustees had resolved to incorporate in the design a single span of iron crossing the water. In short, a bridge that would stay well away from the surging waters of the Severn, and also provide enough height to allow the masts of the Severn trows to pass without trouble.

Visitors to the town were favourably impressed by the new bridge and its burgeoning town of 200 houses and 1,000 inhabitants. They weren't so impressed by the high tolls that were charged to cross the structure; in fact they were reputed to be double the price of others crossing the Severn. But, in 1840, the trustees decided to bring the tolls in line with other toll bridges. Unfortunately I do not have a good picture of the second bridge, but it has been described as being very similar to the one at Ironbridge. The 1806 bridge served the town well for sixty-three years, and at that point, the trustees recognised that it needed replacing due to worn and cracked ironwork. Their decision on design and materials was again to have the third bridge built with iron for the centre section and brick arches for the approaches.

1970s. Looking past the barge locks towards the vinegar factory and power station. (R. Collins)

The third bridge was designed with a much wider road and approaches, and this is the river crossing that we are familiar with today. The construction was carried out by Thomas Vale of Stourport in 1870. Tolls continued to be charged at a halfpenny for pedestrians and four pence for a horse and carriage, though these were abolished in April 1892. Neighbouring Bewdley had done away with its tolls in 1834 as there had been no small competition between the two neighbouring river towns. Bewdley had been the important town for trade in the seventeenth and early eighteenth century, but now Stourport, with its marvellous bridge and canal connection to the industrial Midlands, had eclipsed it medieval rival.

On a personal note, one of the features of the modern bridge that I have always enjoyed is the delightful wrought iron spiral staircase on the eastern side of the bridge made at Bradley's foundry, Kidderminster. As a child, I just had to go up and down it as many times as my father would allow before he got tired and wanted to go home. It is just as popular today, while youngsters still play in and out of the numerous arched approaches as the bridge heads for town, although these days a recently built play area, skateboard arena and paddling pool also keeps them busy.

DEVELOPMENT OF BASINS AND BUILDINGS

In our plan of the town centre (see page 12) we see the street layout as it has been since the nineteenth century, and how those streets, buildings and warehouses are focussed around the canal basins, for it was the basins that brought life and work and thus prosperity to the town. Back in the seventeenth and eighteenth centuries, the River Stour had played a role in the local economy, but that minor waterway was now to be eclipsed after the introduction of the Staffordshire and Worcestershire Canal. Warehouses quickly sprang up around the very first basin (1771) and the river-going trows with their greater carrying capacity were able to gain access via the first wide beam locks. The basin became a transhipment point, as goods were offloaded from trows and loaded into narrowboats, and vice versa, or into a warehouse for storage. Agricultural goods including fruit, grain and hops came from rich farmland all along the banks of the Severn, while iron and industrial goods arrived from the manufacturing centres of Wolverhampton and Birmingham. By 1772 there were working on the wharves around six permanent employees of the S&W Company, and by 1795, at least nine busy warehouses; but there was need for more storage space, plus the necessary wharfage to accommodate the growing number of working boats – a 70ft narrowboat takes up a lot of room.

Originally, as mentioned, there was just one basin, which we know today as the Upper or Middle Basin. This connected to the river via two barge locks with

The Angel, one of the oldest buildings in town, certainly pre-dating the canal.

a small basin in between. Before ten years had gone by, a second basin now called the Clock Basin (due to the installation of a clock in the adjacent warehouse) had been dug. It communicated to the river via two sets of two narrow staircase locks. There was also a small basin between the two locks. As much water was lost from the basins to the river, a pumping engine was employed to top them up. However, by 1805 a river basin had been dug from which a James Watt engine extracted water to maintain the levels in the basins. It was logically called the Engine Basin.

Boat-building and repair took off after 1772, closely associated with the carrying organisations. One of the larger companies was Danks Venn and Company. An advertisement from the early 1800s describes the company as having recently taken over the business from Belsham and Co., and highlighted the operation of their Severn trows. These 60-ton or more vessels sailed twice each week to and from the larger ports of Bristol, Gloucester, Worcester and Bewdley. The company's narrowboats carried all kinds of goods including wines and spirits to not only short-haul destinations in the Black Country, but as far away as Coventry, Leicester, Liverpool, Derby, the Potteries and Manchester. By 1806, the now familiar and loved narrow locks, plus an extra two basins, had been added, while the final Cheapside basin came in 1812, though plans for an additional set of locks never did come to fruition. However a fine business idea never lasts forever, and stiff competition came in the form of the Worcester and Birmingham Canal, which opened for traffic in 1815, bringing an end to Stourport's supremacy.

The town, canal and river traffic prospered for 100 years, but the fortunes of the S&W Canal and that of Stourport were so intertwined that both waxed and waned during the nineteenth century. Around 1881 a local writer found the town:

A sad contrast to its former self. Railways have robbed the Severn and canal of traffic, which now passes by instead of into its commodious basin. We found the company's great commercial hotel 'The Tontine' a large square block, with room sufficient to make up a hundred beds, and equally extensive stabling, diminished to the proportions of one of the smallest Inns in the town. Its extensive rooms being let off to form dwelling houses. One solitary barge, loaded with sand bound for Newport, was the only vessel for the tug 'Athlete'.

The Tontine, Mart Lane Bridge and the Lichfield Basin

These have recently become extremely interesting features for canal enthusiasts and anyone that loves Stourport. The Tontine, built in 1775 with warm red brick sits comfortably on a raised terrace, level with the upper basins, with a fine prospect across the River Severn. It has three storeys, and three wings at the rear (facing the basins) and in the early years boasted a fine ballroom. It was instantly a symbol of the canal company's power and prosperity. A garden was laid out in

Looking up the narrow locks towards the dry dock and small basin; 1950s.

front, between its façade and the river, while two sizeable stables were built next to it to accommodate all the horse-drawn traffic. The Tontine Hotel – named after an archaic form of financing – has gone through four distinct phases in its 200-year history.

For the first 100 years it was a magnificent hotel, built by the canal company to house its higher status employees, entertain its VIP guests, and accommodate travelling merchants. During this period it was named the Arley Inn and later the Stourport Hotel. And then, when the fortunes of the canal and the company waned during the 1840s, it was divided up into ten apartments (called Tontine Cottages) that, by the middle of the twentieth century, were extremely rundown. For the last few decades of the twentieth century The Tontine became a pub, owned and operated by the Wolverhampton and Dudley Breweries. During this period, on a nice summer's day, many hundreds of people milled around its bars or sat on its spacious front lawns and watched the boats go by. At the beginning of the twenty-first century, the pub had lost its appeal and the brewery started to lose money; for a while the fortunes of this grand building were lost in a limbo world, as its windows and doors were firmly boarded up, while the poor unloved structure sat around with a depressed sullen look, awaiting its fate. Fortunately, after some few years passed, developers finally came along with the cash and a vision to turn that historic riparian building back into apartments – again. But this time around they are much more grand affairs – and I have no doubt that the selling prices reflect that upgrade.

You may of course be aware that the canal town of Stourport has in the last few years had a new canal bridge, on Mart Lane, and the reinstatement of a historic basin, besides much ongoing repair work. This is wonderful news for Stourport and of course the canal enthusiast. Right up until the 1950s, the original capacious Lichfield Basin was alive with working boats; its last traffic no doubt included coal to the power station, or products for the vinegar factory, both nearby. Nevertheless, the basin was filled in during the late 1950s and from that time onward the land was used for a variety of purposes, one of those being a wood yard. Before any building work could start, however, an archaeological team was sent along to investigate and record the construction methods of the very early basin, associated buildings and anything else of interest. Of course, they would have loved to have come across remains of one of the Severn trows that sailed the river in the nineteenth century; sadly no such remains were found, but they did find at least three sunken narrowboats. Here is a brief summary of that 2006 archaeological report:

A project of archaeological monitoring and building recording was undertaken at Lichfield Basin, Severn Side, Stourport-on-Severn, Worcestershire (NGR: SO 8110 7100). It was requested by Woodford Land Limited, who intends residential redevelopment for which planning permission has been obtained. The aim of the building recording was to produce a discussion of the history and function of the sail buildings. This should then feed into the research cycle, taking into account local, regional and national research frameworks.

The watching brief of the groundworks revealed the basin, dock and dry dock walls, which comprised brick courses, with occasional timber insertions, sealed by a sandstone block-capping course. Little was identified by way of alteration, with the exception of blocking walls inserted into Cheapside Lock. Few fittings were observed, most notably vertical recessed slots for gates along the inlet from the Upper Basin and a crane base at the corner of the north-west dock. Three very poorly preserved timber vessels of the type known as Joeys or Birmingham Day Boats were exposed within the north-west dock. These were the most common form of un-powered cargo boat in use along the canals of the West Midlands.

Two buildings were recorded, the Sail House in Mart Lane and an adjoining warehouse to the rear. There was no definitive evidence to indicate that the Sail House was ever used for the production or storage of sailcloth, although the building is known locally as 'The Sail House' and there are suggestions that it was once a sailcloth and tarpaulin workshop. The building, which was described as a warehouse in 1810, dates from the late eighteenth century with modifications over the following century and a half. A narrow building, which was probably open to the rear, was built onto the Sail House in the mid-nineteenth century. This was enclosed when the warehouse was constructed on the eastern side of the Sail House in the early twentieth century. The aim of the building recording was to record fixtures and fittings within the warehouse, and to produce a discussion of the history and function of the Sail House.

The aim of the watching brief was to observe areas of ground disturbance associated with construction and to record archaeological structures, horizons, features and deposits associated with the extant buildings, to determine their extent, state of preservation, date and type, as far as reasonably possible. In particular the watching brief aimed to record the structure of the canal basin: the walls, accesses, fixtures and associated structures and any buried historic vessels (boats), especially Droitwich trows.

The report was indeed a long one, but I have summarised the salient information by noting that the Lichfield Basin was all of one piece, or in other words there were no clearly defined breaks or alterations in the brickwork to suggest different phases of construction or repairs. The basins' walls generally comprised a single upper course of sandstone quay stones, 1ft deep, laid over a course of blue engineering bricks. The wall was generally four bricks wide in the upper courses, and up to the considerable width of seven bricks elsewhere.

2010: In between the two sets of narrow locks with the engine house in the distance. (James Watt)

The wall thickness was not the only impressive dimension. The basin itself was up to 10ft 6in deep, reducing to 8ft at the northern docks, and 7ft 6in at the dry docks. The middle dry dock was back filled as early as 1903, and in 1927 a building was put upon it. During the nineteenth century the basin was used for general goods, but from 1927 to 1949 it was the terminus for boats on what was termed 'The Light Run', bringing many tons of coal to the town's power station. In 1949, the station began to receive coal from a new railway, and the basin was slowly filled in.

So, what of the three day boats that were discovered buried in the north-west dock? The report states that they were common Birmingham day boats (Joeys), unpowered, double-ended cargo boats, either open or with a single cabin at the stern. They were similar in construction to the much earlier Worsley mine boats, which are considered to be the forerunner of the narrowboat, and were also called 'starvationers' because of the exposed rib construction. Such vessels were built in their thousands during the nineteenth and early twentieth century, making them the most common boat on the canals of the West Midlands. Built of wood, iron or steel, in a combination, they varied in size and capacity according to builder, company or cargo specifications; but a standard 70ft by 6ft 6in boat could in theory load up to 40 tons with a draft of 3ft 10in, but this was more like 25–30 tons in practice.

As part of the archaeological record, a 'Building Record' was drawn up. Perhaps the most curious item near the Lichfield Basin is the intriguingly called 'Sail House' on Mart Lane. There was no definite evidence to indicate that it was ever used for the production or storage of sailcloth, but locals believe that it was once a sailcloth and tarpaulin workshop. The building was described as a warehouse in 1810, and dates from the late eighteenth century, receiving modifications over the ensuing years. Stourport is rich in such pieces of architecture, and most worthy of a visit. Stourport Civic Society, Stourport Forward and British Waterways have together produced a fine heritage trail with useful accompanying leaflets.

The Lichfield Basin

This is the really interesting feature for canal enthusiasts. The Lichfield Basin – also known in the past as the 'Furthermost' or the 'New' Basin – was constructed by the canal company in 1806. It connected to the Middle Basin by means of a channel under Mart Lane Bridge, which was also lost in the 1950s. The basin

The Furthermost or Lichfield Basin as it appeared in the 1950s before being filled in.

Plan of the original Lichfield Basin, and its modern successor. Notice that the later 2006 basin is much smaller than its predecessor.

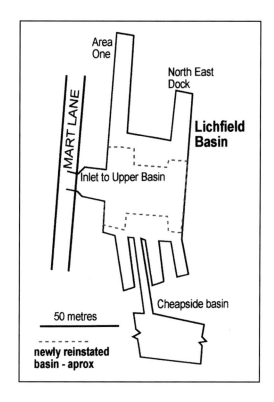

Area One

North East Dock

MART LANE

Lichfield Basin

Inlet to Upper Basin

Cheapside basin

50 metres

- - - - - - - -
newly reinstated basin - aprox

had five arms and a further connection to another basin at Cheapside via a lock. Used by both Severn trows and narrowboats, its final use was during the 1950s by coal companies such as T.S. Elements, who brought thousands of tons of coal into the southern corner ready for transhipment to the power station only a few hundred yards along the river. Though the basin was filled in during the 1950s, to become first a gasworks and later a wood yard, there were rumours for several decades that it would be reinstated. Now the rumours have been turned aside for the concrete reality of a revival. The project, completed in 2011, included the reinstatement of the basin, but without its arms. Plans were drawn up in 2006, to restore the basin along with extremely attractive and original-looking Mart Lane Bridge; and a lengthy architectural study was undertaken to take a note of the original building techniques, and to see if any interesting remains were to be found under the many tons of backfill. In 2007, work on the basin and Mart Lane Bridge was started. Moorings were included in the design for a dozen or so narrowboats, while the basin itself would be surrounded by attractive and hopefully desirable residential properties. Not only would this grant an enormous visual enhancement to the already wonderful water features of Stourport, but it would also provide a greater reservoir of water for boats going up and down the two sets of locks. The whole process of redevelopment of the town and its basins during the latter decade of the twentieth and first decade of the twenty-first centuries was fascinating to observe.

Associated with those worthy goals were other objectives that included a desire to increase the number of day visitors to the town, and thus attract an increase in visitor spending to the local economy to the projected figure of £1.7 million. British Waterways also added interpretive features around the site so that visitors can gain an appreciation of how important the canal features were to the birth and growth of the town. In future years there will be an events programme designed to attract thousands of additional tourists, and hopefully this will result in the creation of many new jobs. Funding for the restoration work, which I hasten to add did not include the restoration of the Lichfield Basin, was £3,171,687, and specifically included nearly £1.5 million going to the existing basins, £51,000 for conservation work and £25,500 for archaeological recording. Other monies went to marketing, tourism and community development to make up the total.

If asked if Stourport needed all that attention, then the only answer must be yes. Stourport's birth was a direct result of the construction of the Staffordshire and Worcestershire Canal, its early basins, locks and buildings, and the continued development and maintenance of those features are essential for its future.

The new Lichfield Basin under construction in 2006.

The basin completed and watered; 2008.

WAREHOUSES

During the nineteenth century, when carrying activity was at its height, Stourport's basins were flanked by warehouses. In the early years, iron was the main commodity, but as time passed by every kind of merchandise passed through the basins including foodstuffs, timber-building materials, clay for the potteries, manufactured goods and, of course, coal. Many of those buildings were destroyed during the first half of the twentieth century but three remain, and they are the iron room – also used as the Canal Company offices; the Clock warehouse built in 1812; and the building close to York Street Lock which is now used as the Chandlery. Fortunately we still have some great black and white prints depicting those warehouses.

PLANS FOR STOURPORT THROUGH THE YEARS

In 1909, the Royal Commission recommended that the Severn be improved to take a 600-ton craft as far as Stourport, though the 1914 war came along to put an end to those plans. But Stourport was by no means down and out; there were regular consignments of aluminium, oil traffic to just below the town during the first half of the twentieth century, and also many dozens of narrowboats that hauled Staffordshire coal to the town's power station.

Then from the 1950s onward, Stourport reinvented itself as a place to be visited in its own right. This time it wasn't the upper echelons of Georgian society who came in their elegant horse-drawn carriages, but thousands of workers from the Black Country who arrived in their Ford Anglias and Morris Minors. Their children took rides on the funfair, before the whole family rode downriver on one of the pleasure boats, finishing the day off with fish and chips from the High Street, or a pint from the Tontine or Angel. The river and basins became the seaside equivalent of the promenade, where today groups of day-trippers continue to dawdle around the locks for the innocent pleasure of watching the black dripping chambers fill and empty, and boats enter or leave the basins. As the twentieth century progressed, so did the ideas for the town and its canal heritage. In August 1995, Pieda PLC, a consultancy organisation, was approached by British Waterways and the Wyre Forest District Council to prepare a regeneration strategy for the whole town. The purpose clearly understood and stated in their document was to make the very best use of the heritage of the town, to encourage tourism and provide for the long-term economic benefit of not just the town, but the surrounding district too.

The report noted that Stourport was well known as a popular day trip and short-term destination that focussed on leisure and commercial tourism – nothing new there then – and that the key attractions were the riverside gardens, Shipley's Leisure Park (which has had a long and prosperous association with the town) riverboat trips, and the canal basins, that included the Tontine and Clock warehouse as important historical pieces of architecture in their own right. Indeed, as many of us Midlanders already knew, Stourport has always been an inexpensive pleasurable place to motor to. Many of us just went there for the day, but many others purchased riverside caravans, and the parks opposite the town grew extensively from the 1960s onward. I remember staying in a caravan opposite the power station during the 1960s, at which time there was just a single ring of caravans surrounding an open field. But today, that site is home to a whole regiment of posh metal boxes, and I believe that the character of the old days has somehow been sadly lost. Funding for developments was then sought through partnerships with other interested bodies, and plans were afoot to reinstate one of the lost basins. While Shipley's, who ran the fair, intended to invest £2 million in an all-weather, all-year-round leisure complex.

STOURPORT'S CHARACTERS

The town has never been short of its grand characters, and some have had a great import on its canal and river scene. During the 1920s, Stourport's basins and

Construction of the new Mart Lane Bridge, sympathetic to the original which allowed access to the Lichfield Basin; 2006.

Completion of the bridge, note that some of the new residential properties around the basin have also been finished; 2009.

Completed buildings on the north of the basin; 2011.

Stourport's most recent river bridge.

Close up of the bridge, spiral staircase, and access along the river.

Shipley's Fairground, one of the oldest established fairs in the country.

The Tea Rooms at York Street Lock; in the distance is the nineteenth-century Toll Office.

The proprietor of the Tea Rooms has a fascinating collection of mid-twentieth-century memorabilia; well worth a look.

wharves were in a bad way, and it was George Cadbury of chocolate fame who stepped in to improve matters. First he modernised the boats and dock facilities, then he persuaded the dock company to reduce their charges, and followed that up by running a publicity campaign to promote the waterways.

Holt Abbott

Holt Abbott was an electrical engineer during the Second World War who worked on secret anti-submarine equipment. After the war he bought a boat and lived on it at Saul and Worcester before coming to Stourport, where, in 1946, he met Tom and Angela Rolt, Robert Aickman and Peter Scott aboard *Cressy*. The former were sowing the seeds of the early Inland Waterway Association (IWA), but they also influenced Abbott, who was motivated by Rolt's book *Narrow Boat* to start building cruising boats to his own design and specifications.

Looking across the upper basin to Aaron York's house; 2010.

The Sail House on Mart Lane; formerly a warehouse.

Looking up Stourport's High Street away from the basins and river during the early twentieth century.

His company was called Canal Pleasurecraft and he operated firstly out of the Middle Basin and later from the British Waterways depot on the canal approach to York Street Lock. He turned out more than thirty boats until his retirement in 1979, when he sold out to Dartline. Holt Abbott was a founder member of the IWA and one of the first to initiate the leisure boat movement.

INDUSTRIES AND POWER STATION

From the 1840s onward, industries continued to move into the town, where cheap land and access to the river and canal proved a great inducement. These included a tannery, foundry, gasworks, a carpet and a vinegar factory. All of these activities of course added to the population, and also to the success of the town and its canal. Added to that traffic was an enormous amount of coal. This was boated down the S&W for the benefit of the huge coal-fired power station just below the mouth of the Stour. Opened by Stanley Baldwin in 1928, this colossal structure with its towering chimneys was for many decades a profound feature of the Stourport landscape, and an important source of electrical power. When I and my family went along to Stourport for holidays during the 1960s, I was fascinated by the sight of the whole of the station, chimneys and all, being covered in a camouflage colour scheme that was used to deter German bombers during the Second World War. I suppose that its possible destruction could have caused quite a problem in the area, though I doubt whether the Luftwaffe ever came near it. The station drew its cooling waters straight from the Stour, and then deposited the same into the Severn, though several degrees warmer – the fish loved it.

Though few people will admit to feeling the loss of such a structure, there is no doubt that the power station had an interesting architectural façade, and was the main source of traffic after the First World War on the southern half of the S&W, mainly by T.S. Elements. Ironically, when the previously mentioned Stanley Baldwin officiated at the opening of the power station, he pointed out in his speech that in his youth he had played cricket on that exact location; and I can report that some six decades later he could carry on playing, as the station was demolished during the 1980s, and the land soon after reverted to a green field alongside the river; the only tell-tale sign being the concrete frontage along the riverbank.

During the nineteenth century, the canal settlement grew into a town with a high street, shopping and community facilities. New businesses were also attracted to a site that had the advantage of both river and canal transport. Among the newcomers were the Anglo American Tin Stamping Company, a gasworks, carpet factory, vinegar works, petroleum depot, and the Steatite & Porcelain Products Co. Other enterprises that had previously existed on a family-run basis such as the tannery and iron works also saw great expansion.

Perhaps one of the most unusual of those was the vinegar works, which I personally recall in the 1960s as giving a distinct aroma to the riverside. In a *History of the Town and Area* by Anne Bradford, the author writes of a certain Hicken Bold, whose remains lie in Mitton churchyard. Bold was the founder of what eventually came to be the world-famous firm of Holbrook's. During their early years they produced only malt vinegar, but soon went on to make several sauces. The company went through a rollercoaster ride of expansion and at least two disastrous fires until they were taken over by Sarsons in 1954. The company closed in 2000. Like many of the companies mentioned, Holbrook's made much use of the canal and river for the delivery of raw materials and finished goods until, like so many others, they succumbed to the use of either rail or road transport.

Certainly, the land around Lower Mitton has experienced many alterations since the 1770s, as the location passed through three distinct phases. The early farming community, the busy interchange port of canal and river, and more recently its leisure/tourist phase. Just before I finish, I must mention one other place of interest. At York Street Lock, one will find that the adjacent building is finely situated as a café. What most passers-by do not realise is that inside that café, the owner – who is a bit of a collector and historian – has a small but fascinating museum of everyday objects from the early twentieth century. And if

Winter at
Stourport's Upper
Basin 2010,
with the clock
warehouse in the
distance.

you are of a certain age, you will probably delight in the objects on display as you
partake of a cup of tea and a sandwich.

2

Josiah Wedgwood: His Contribution to the Waterways

Josiah Wedgwood was a man that came to be loved and admired by his own generation. Today, Josiah Wedgwood is an inspirational model for anyone who wants to triumph over adversity and continually strive for improvements. Wedgwood hauled himself up from a humble and painful childhood to set fine standards in the field of pottery, and en route he became one of the most important promoters for Britain's canals. What, then, were his beginnings, what sort of privations did he suffer, and how did he become intimately connected with James Brindley, the Duke of Bridgwater, and other noteworthies who gave so much impetus to the Industrial Revolution? First we need to understand the kind of conditions around Burslem when Josiah was a boy.

Josiah was born in 1730, the youngest of thirteen children. He entered an environment that was a kind of dynasty of potters, though it must be said on a small scale. His father, Thomas Wedgwood, was one of a clan of Wedgwoods living in Staffordshire. He had a small works known as the Churchyard Pottery in Burslem near Stoke-on-Trent, where he employed about six men. This was not the refined sort of pottery that went into

Josiah Wedgwood; Master Potter.

Site of the Brownhills, where the very first section of the Trent and Mersey began in 1766. (Sandwell Libraries)

the fine houses of the day. At Burslem they turned out such common household items as soup and porridge dishes and other kitchenware.

At the age of seven, Josiah went to a small informal school, kept by a Mr Blunt, to learn his elementary ABCs, but he was not there long, for his father died when he was nine. Fortunately he possessed an inner motivation that drove him to essentially educate himself. Books were the means to knowledge for Josiah, as they were for others who had a hunger for information and wanted to improve their lot in life. For two years he had been occupied at what was now his brother's pottery works, and young Josiah had a gift and love for making clay models. His older brother was apparently unimpressed with his early artistic prowess. However, at the age of only eleven, Josiah's endurance was to be severely tested.

SMALLPOX IN BURSLEM

In 1741 there was an outbreak of smallpox in Burslem and Josiah, along with many others, became extremely ill. For a long period the boy was not strong enough to get out of bed, and though he eventually did recover, his convalescence took many months and his health was never the same. At length he got up and used crutches, but the virus had permanently damaged his knee, and he would suffer continual pain and poor eyesight throughout his life. (After an accident much later in life, he was in so much pain, that he actually had his leg amputated without the benefit of any anaesthetic.) However as a lad, he eventually went back to throwing pots and became quite skilful, entering into an apprenticeship. At the age of twenty he inherited £20; not a lot of money, but at least it gave him a start. As the years went by Josiah had a succession of partnerships and his business grew steadily. But to understand how he became involved in a big way with the planning and building of the inland waterway system, we need to understand what conditions were like in Burslem during the first half of the eighteenth century.

STAFFORDSHIRE TRANSPORT

The Staffordshire of that day had a shortage of roads, and those that did exist were rough dirt bridleways full of rocks and puddles. The inland situation of the potters at Burslem was worse than inconvenient, and though some of the clay was close at hand, the only way to get their pots to market was on the back of the pack horses that lumbered and stumbled along the trackways. The poor horses, urged on by the lash, stumbled through the mud and often fell, upsetting their small loads, causing many breakages. If they broke a leg, they were shot where they fell. To correct this intolerable situation, Josiah attempted to improve the road system, but there were many that objected. Josiah's transport objectives were the port of Liverpool on the west coast, that would serve not only Britain but also America, and the port of Hull on the east coast, that would serve interests in

A stylized view of the Wedgwood Works at Etruria, Stoke on Trent, that came to be a popular illustration on the company's pottery ware. (Sandwell Libraries)

Europe. There had to be a better way of getting his valuable but fragile goods to these two ports.

The idea of a navigation between these two towns had already been alluded to. The Duke of Bridgewater had just built his Worsley to Manchester Canal in 1761. Wedgwood had known James Brindley for some time, because that gentleman had been involved in building a mill for the grinding of flint in Staffordshire. The construction of a canal was an enormous undertaking, but Wedgwood knew that if anyone could accomplish this waterway, Brindley could. He was already known as 'the schemer' and had constructed what for that time was an amazing feat, an aqueduct over the Irwell that had been nicknamed 'The Castle in the Air'.

RELATIONSHIP WITH THE DUKE OF BRIDGEWATER

Wedgwood came to have such a close association with the Duke of Bridgewater that he wrote on 6 July 1765:

> I have been waiting upon his Grace the Duke of Bridgewater with plans respecting inland navigation. Mr Sparrow went along with me. We were most graciously received; we spent about eight hours in his Grace's company and had all the assurances of his concurrence in our designs that we could wish. His Grace gave me

Photograph of the Etruria works before demolition during the middle of the twentieth century. The cupola housed a bell that called the men and women to work.

The dining room at Matthew Boulton's house in Birmingham, where members of what we now call the Lunar Society met, including Josiah Wedgwood, James Watt and Erasmus Darwin. The house is today a fine visitor attraction, and it is fascinating to be in the actual room where these illustrious men met for dinner and socialising. If only walls could talk …

an order for the complete set of table service of cream-colour that I could make. He showed us a Roman urn, 1500 years old at least made of red china, which had been found by his workmen in Castle Field near Manchester. After his Grace had dismissed us we had the honour and pleasure of sailing on his gondola some 9 miles along his canal, through a most delightful vale to Manchester.

The first public movement in support of Brindley's survey occurred in December 1765, when an open-air meeting was held at Wolsley Bridge. Attending were the big names of Earl Gower, Lord Grey, Mr Bagot, Mr Anson, Mr Gilbert and of course Wedgwood and Brindley. The plans were fully discussed, adopted, and it was resolved to obtain the necessary Act of Parliament. Wedgwood with his usual generosity subscribed £1,000 towards the preliminary expenses and also promised to subscribe for a sizeable proportion of the shares. The main promoters of the scheme were originally going to name it 'The canal from the Trent to the Mersey',

Wedgwood's house as it is in more recent years. Etruria Hall was built on rising ground between 1768 and 1771 to a design by Joseph Pickford. The Wedgwood family moved in on completion. But, as the family increased in size, extensions were planned, and in 1780, two wings, two storeys high joined by a single corridor were added. Wedgwood died at the hall in 1795, a multi-millionaire by any modern standards, and was buried at Stoke church. The house was sold by the Wedgwood family during the 1840s and is now a hotel.

but Brindley knew that this canal would be only the start of a much larger project that would eventually connect up with other waterways, and he wisely suggested that they call it 'The Grand Trunk'.

WAR OF THE PAMPHLETS

The Staffordshire potters were delighted, and the following day they had a bonfire at Burslem where they drank the health of the promoters. But just as there had been opponents of the road schemes, there were many who bitterly objected to the canals proposals, especially the owners of the Weaver Navigation who didn't want to lose the great advantage they already enjoyed. Both sides went to war with pamphlets. Wedgwood's group was entitled 'A View of the Advantages of Inland Navigation, with a Plan of a Navigable canal intended for a communication between the ports of Liverpool and Hull'.

The promoters had a battle of the pamphlets on their hands, however, they knew that the real difficulty was going to be getting the waterway over or through the high ground at Harecastle. This was where Brindley's confidence and natural zeal shone through. The battle of the pamphlets moved to tough verbal exchanges in Parliament, but the promoters had some big guns on their side and eventually the project went through on 14 May 1766. There were more rejoicings at Burslem, and the first sod was dug by Wedgwood on 26 July that summer. Wedgwood's leg was so bad at that time that Brindley barrowed the earth away amidst loud cheers. At a meeting of the proprietors Wedgwood was appointed treasurer, demonstrating the esteem in which he was held. Brindley's salary was fixed at £200 per annum, but Wedgwood was worried about his friend for he wrote to Mr Bentley in March 1767; 'I am afraid Brindley is endeavouring to do too much, and that he will leave us before his vast designs are accomplished. He is so incessantly harassed on every side that he hath no rest for either mind or body, and he will not be prevailed upon to take proper care of his health.' Later in March he wrote again on a similar subject. His admiration for Brindley was great, but he also recognised that the man was only going to an early grave if he continued with the same punishing work schedule.

At one of the first committee meetings, the newly formed canal company ordered that work should start at both ends of the proposed Harecastle tunnel – a project that was not to be finished for eleven years. Yet through all those years Wedgwood stuck firmly to his resolve in order that the problems for the potters of Staffordshire would finally be solved. In the meanwhile he built his famous works of Etruria right on the banks of the new canal, ensuring that raw materials could be boated in from as far away as Cornwall, and that finished goods could reach the world.

3

Charlie Foster: The Story of a Real Boatman

THE 1920S

In the late 1920s, as a boy of eight, I used to go with different members of my family on the boats. They carried coal from the coalfields all over the country to factories and coal wharves. During these years, the crews worked long hours, and most of the boats were horse-drawn. In my school holidays I used to go with my brothers, and spent much of the time on the towing path driving the horses. And, as the years went by, I seemed to get the call of the canal in my blood, and thoroughly enjoyed my time there. Nevertheless, because the working hours were very long, I thought it wise on leaving school to take an office job. Maybe it wasn't so wise after all.

After three months with a company, I requested to go to night school for study, but one day while walking home for lunch, Ernie Thomas (a well-known Walsall Canal carrier) drew up in his car and gave me a lift home, as I lived in a house on his coal wharf. My father at this time was his horse fettler and foreman. While in the car, Ernie asked me if I would like to work for him on one of his towing tugs. This proposition pleased me no end, and I started the following week. My time in an office had been a short one.

The first boat I went on was the *Tiny*, and I was mate to Len Wilson who was the driver. Our first jobs were travelling from our base at Walsall top lock over to Aldridge Colliery, waiting while the boat loaders filled the four boats with slack – shovelling it off the backs of rail trucks – and then towing them to Walsall power station. These working days were usually about twelve to fourteen hours' long. Once at the power station the boats were all emptied by overhead grabs, and we were then ready for a repeat trip. After six months, I was transferred to another tug and driver, and we did trips from the Hednesford and Cannock collieries.

Birchill's power station, 1958. Ernie Thomas of Walsall had the coal delivery contract. Coal came from Holly Bank pit. (J. Haddock)

This was transporting coal and slack to the tar works in Oldbury. After a year doing this on the motor boats I decided that it would be nice to have a change, so I went to work with my uncle, Charlie Bates from Tividale, who worked horseboats for the Oldbury-based firm of Kimberley Beddows.

My two brothers also worked for this company, and it wasn't long before I was working with the eldest. Now, I was boating from Oldbury to Hednesford and back, taking slack to Danks's Boiler Works, Brades Steel, and the Patent Shaft and Axle Works in Wednesbury. During the 1930s there were many boats on the BCN, and we often had to wait ages at the locks as there could be as many as twenty boats at the top or bottom of each flight. Also during these years there were as many as 150 horseboats each day on the Cannock Extension Canal alone. It was a very busy waterway.

On 9 December 1937, we experienced one of those extremely foggy days when you couldn't see more than 20 yards in front of your nose, and as dusk came on, things got even worse. First the horse fell in, and later on so did I, and my brother. Fortunately we were able to clamber out, but sadly the horse drowned, which was distressing to both of us. We found some kind assistance from one of the nearby houses, and the family were good enough to let us have a

Freddy Moore working Ernie Thomas's boat *Enterprise* on the W&E Canal in 1966. (J. Haddock)

Early twentieth century at Ernie Thomas's yard, Walsall. Tom Foster – Charlie's father and Horace's grandfather (right of picture) – was horse fettler and yard foreman for Ernie Thomas.

bath and change of clothes. My brother then telephoned someone who would be able to contact my father, and as all the buses were off due to the fog, they walked to meet us at Perry Bar. When we were all together at about five in the morning, my father and brothers went to sort out the horse, but I was still too upset to go along to drag our horse from the murky waters of the canal.

After a couple of weeks off work I first went as mate to my uncle, as two of my brothers were now working as a pair, and then some time later I came into contact with my third brother who was still working for Ernie Thomas − you see, boating really was a family affair. He told me that his mate was leaving and would I consider going back to Thomas's. Well, in those days you quickly weighed up who was paying the best wages, and it didn't take me too long to make my mind up to return to the yard at Walsall Top Lock. So now we were collecting coal from Hampstead Colliery on the Tame Valley Canal and boating it to Lester Brothers at Acocks Green on the Grand Union. This voyage, going from one side of Birmingham to the other, involved working fifty locks each day and a round trip of some 20 miles. I was back doing twelve to fourteen hours a day. I worked this routine until the war broke out in 1939, when Ernie swapped us round on to other jobs.

THE WAR YEARS

I was now boating to lots of different places, and because everyone was putting in a special effort for the war, we even boated through the night. This included the nights when air raids were on and bombs were dropping all around Birmingham. Of course we were not allowed to show any lights and believe me, horseboating at night in the dark takes some getting used to. As the war went on, the raids got worse, so the canal company decided that it was best to put stop planks at certain positions so that if a bomb did hit the banks, the loss of water would be limited. This policy meant of course that we could now only travel between 6 a.m. and 6 p.m., which forced us to spend two or three nights a week away from home. And just like the long-distance boatmen, we now slept in our tiny cabins. Of course we had the advantage of free coal, so we kept our stoves going.

The government and the local authorities did everything they could to keep the wheels of industry turning. During the winter of 1940, and not long after the famous Battle of Britain, we had another battle to contend with – the battle against ice on the cut. Canal transport was vital, so many of us went to work on the iceboats.

These boats were narrow and short, and plated with metal on the outside of the hull for protection against the ice. The boats were again pulled by horses, not just one, but up to twenty. A dozen or more men got on the iceboat and stood holding a thick rope that was fixed between two short masts. They would then rock the boat from side to side as they were pulled into the ice sheets. The horses were often run at a gallop, so it was a dangerous and exciting operation. The bad weather lasted eight to ten weeks, and everyone was glad, especially the bosses, when the thaw finally came.

At work, there was the occasional dispute, and my brother Horace and I had a particular grievance with the boss Ernie Thomas, and so I left to work with

Charlie Foster on the W&E with his children. Notice the bag of horse feed on top of the coal.

Charlie Foster on the *Princess Anne* at Perry Bar.

Portrait of Charlie and Vera Foster
during the 1940s.

my uncle again. One afternoon in the October of 1941, whilst returning from a delivery of slack to the General Electricity Company at Witton, my brother fell into one of the Perry Bar locks and drowned at the age of 32. After that, one of my cousins came to work with me until 1943. Some time later, my uncle lost some horseboat work so he decided to move to J. Holloway, who were running motor boats along the Wyrley and Essington Canal. Meanwhile my other two brothers, Tom and Bill, were now working for the boat builder and repairer Peter Keay, who also did canal transport. Men were always on the move in those days from one company to another if they could improve their pay and conditions, so I went to join Bill. We were still moving coal, but this time it was to pastures new. We were collecting as in the past from the East Cannock Colliery, but taking it to the Stuart Glass Company in Stourbridge on the other side of the Rowley Ridge.

Starting on Monday morning, we used to travel from Pratt's Bridge (Walsall), from where Keay operated, to Cannock with an empty boat, collect a 28-ton loaded boat at the colliery and bring it back to Walsall Bottom lock; end of day one. Tuesday morning we would start the second half of the journey via the Tipton and Factory locks, Netherton Tunnel, Delph locks, and finally the Stourbridge sixteen. On arrival at Stuart's we would then have to empty the coal from the boat onto their wharf with shovels. This alone would take about three and a half hours. After unloading, it was then time to take the horse to the stable and feed and groom it. Finally we had some time to ourselves, and we would cook a meal and then go along to the Stuart's Social Club for a hard earned hour or two.

Occasionally we went into the heat of the glass cone to watch the glass blowers at work. The men would be arranged around the central furnace in teams, gathering, working and blowing the glass items, and we always found this interesting. Sometimes if they felt generous, they would make us an ornament, a jug or maybe a few glasses to hang in the cabin. Then we would grab some sleep in the boat before heading back up the Stourbridge and Delph locks to Walsall. Next morning would be the start of a new journey. Today I would get the horse out of the stable while Bill made a cup of tea, and then we would set off for Littleton Colliery, again via the Dudley and Stourbridge, but this time carrying on to Stourton and then right onto the Staffordshire and Worcestershire Canal. It was then north up the S&W as far as Otherton Basin, where we dropped off the empty and swapped our gear on to a loaded boat that was full of what was called 'washed cobbles' – there were lots of different types of coal. It was then off south to Aldersley, up the 21 to Wolverhampton and on to a brass factory at Winson Green via Bilston, Tipton and West Bromwich. Thankfully there was no unloading; we just dropped off the full and returned with an empty.

Charlie Foster steering the *Princess Anne* during the 1960s.

Perry Bar locks – known as Jules to the boatmen. The General ELectric Comapny is in the background where a delivery of coal has just been made.

In 1943, during the middle of the war years, we went on to a new contract. This entailed four voyages each week from East Cannock Colliery to Smith, Stone and Knights Paper Mills in Saltley. For the final years of the war, we were on many and varied contracts, which all kept the job interesting and enjoyable. In 1945, I was tempted to go and work for the Birmingham firm of T.S. Elements, who advertised themselves as Haulage and Steering Contractors. They too had a wide variety of contracts with differing journeys, and scenic routes like the aforementioned Staffs and Worcs run. A local BCN run was picking up 28-ton coal boats from the Oozell's Street basin and taking them to the Yardley Co-op coal yard. You could do one trip per day, but it was a tiring job. Tugs would drop the boats off at Oozell's Street, and we would pick them up at 6 a.m.; pass through the Farmers bridge flight, and on to Ashted and Camp Hill. We usually arrived at about twelve o'clock. After tying the horse to the fence and feeding him, we emptied the boat and made our way back to Oozell's Street for roughly 6.30 p.m.

BAD WINTERS

The winter of 1946 was bad for everyone, and thick snow built over equally thick ice from the November of that year right through to April 1947. I joined others on the iceboats, but this only worked for a while and then everything was solidly frozen into the banks. T.S. Elements were forward thinking, and had purchased some lorries which they used for City Council contract work. And I did some work with these, helping to grit and salt the roads. Eventually the thaw came, and we were back to the boats, but there was a noticeable difference. Coal mines, wharves, and various other industries were continuing to close down as the coal trade either slowed or moved to road and rail transport, and the government decided to nationalise the waterways. As a consequence of this I decided to go long-distance boating and applied to the new British Waterways.

My first trips were transporting cement from Southam up to Camphill in Birmingham; three trips per week. A few weeks down the line we had a problem with the motorboat, which put it out of action for almost three weeks. So, British Waterways arranged for us to take two loads down the Grand Union to Nash Paper Mills. We loaded up at Pooley Hall Colliery, and this job entailed a boat swap at Bulls Bridge, where the company had a large depot. But I didn't come straight back, as my mate decided to quit canal work; so the foremen put me on the dock for a few weeks to see if a mate could be found. Things didn't seem to be working out at British Waterways, and I ended up returning to Ernie Thomas. He still had a lot of work transporting slack to power stations. By this time, many of the horseboats had been replaced by motors and butties, and I went to work a pair, shifting coal from Anglesey basin to Ocker Hill power station.

Charlie Foster with his own leisure boat *Vulcan*, which he owned from 1971-1985.

On the Daw End branch during the 1960s. The *Princess Anne* with Charlie in front with 23 tons, towing Horace on the first butty and Bill on the third, both carrying 28 tons.

Manually hauling the coal boat into Longwood Lock, early morning, heading for Witton.

Things went well for a while until the day that the gaffer promised us that we would be soon having a brand new boat. And then, when the boat arrived, he gave it to another pair, so me and my mate speedily put our notice in, and I went back to T.S. Elements. But as I mentioned earlier, we boatmen could see the writing on the wall as far as canal carrying was concerned. Fortunately Elements had other contracts such as regularly taking rubbish from a variety of firms over to Moxley on the Walsall Canal. Also there was plenty of repair work to places such as the Cannock Extension Canal which was then suffering from considerable land subsidence – due of course to the extensive mining activity in the area.

1950-1967

During these years I went through a succession of different mates who decided, after boating for a while, that the long hours were not worth doing. And then a chap came out of the army who had been a boatman before. He was already mentally and physically prepared for the job, and as we lived fairly close, it turned out to be a good partnership. We started by doing five journeys each week from Pooley Hall Colliery to the GEC at Witton. This was a sixteen-hour trip, and didn't include cycling to Salford Bridge every morning as this was where Elements had their second base of operations. Later we managed to cut the travel time when we started delivering to factories closer to Walsall. But, after a while, even he left for a better job in Tipton, and I was forced to try out some school leavers without much success. So, in 1954, I applied for and got a job at Samuel Barlow LTD of Braunston. My first pair of boats was the *Tiger* and the butty *Mary*.

My first journey was taking cobbles from Longford Coventry to what everyone called the 'Jam Ole' factory on the Paddington Arm. Once there, it was time to empty the boat, but as the grab had broken, it was all done by muscle and shovel. From there it was back to Braunston with the empty, where we changed the *Tiger* for the *Beatty*, as the lighting system on the *Tiger* had packed up on us. This had caused some concerns as we came back through the long Grand Union tunnels. Both motors used the 12hp Petter hot bulb start engines, but the *Beatty* was steel while the *Tiger* had been wood.

The next morning after another change of boats, we were off to Newdigate Colliery to load with slack for the Ovaltine works at Kings Langley. This round trip took exactly one week. This working away from home was not good for a married man, so I returned to Peter Keay in Walsall as a tug driver. The tug often hauled five loaded boats from the mines over to first Wolverhampton, and then carrying on to Birmingham with the remaining three. But the coal contract

T.S. Elements boats including the *Queen Mary* at Elements boat dock at Oldbury. (Keith Hodgkins)

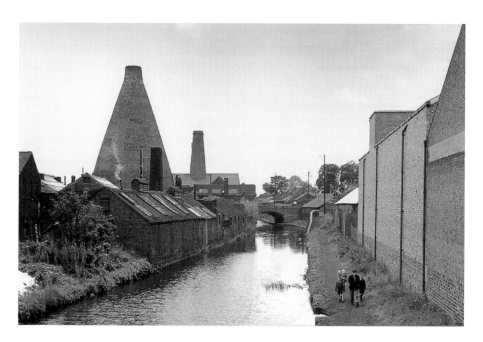

Stuart Glass during the 1960s. Charlie brought regular loads of coal to this wharf from the Cannock Collieries. (Keith Hodgkins)

Charlie Foster on the cover of National Geographic magazine.

Horace Foster at The Bratch; 2010.

continued to dry up, so I made a last move back to Elements, where I did my final years of boating.

While I was there, my son Horace came to work alongside me as soon as he left school. We used to boat from Walsall Wood Colliery, where we loaded by shovel from the trucks, and then delivered the slack to Wilmot Breedon at Haymills near

Yardley. This was two journeys each week. Road transport soon put an end to that job, so we then took slack to the GEC with the horseboats, after which we moved on to the motor *Princess Anne*. This boat carried a load, and towed two butties, usually to the GEC, but occasionally there was a load to the Birmingham Science Museum, which in those days was half way up the Farmers Bridge flight. Washed cobbles went into the boiler house. I then recall Holly Bank Colliery closing, so we collected coal from Anglesey basin. Here the boats were loaded from lorries down a chute, which saved a lot of manual labour. Horace and I worked up to 1967, when the pit told us that there would be no more loads, and that they had already gone twelve months over the contract. When we arrived back at the GEC, George Element was waiting with our redundancy notice, and that was the end of my life as a commercial boatman.

A TRUE LIFE STORY

IN THE LATE TWENTIES AS BOY OF EIGHT I USED TO GO WITH DIFFERENT ONE'S OF MY FAMILIES ON THE CANAL BOATS WHICH FETCHED COAL FROM THE COALFIELDS IN ALL PARTS OF THE COUNTRY TO FACTORIES AND COAL WHARVES ELSEWHE. AT THIS TIME HORSES WERE USED FOR THE PULLING OF THE BOATS AND USED TO WORK VERY LONG HOURS.

IN MY SCHOOL HOLIDAYS I USED TO SPEND MY TIME GOING WITH MY BROTHERS ON THIER JOURNEYS · SO THAT I COULD DRIVE THE HORSES ON THE TOWING PATHS.

AS THE YEARS PASSED BY I GOT THE CALL OF THE CANALS IN MY BLOOD BUT ON BECOMING SCHOOL LEAVING AGE I DECIDED I WOULDN'T DO THAT TYPE OF WORK OWING TO THE LONG HOURS AND VERY LOW WAGES I SETTLED TO WORK IN AN OFFICE.

NEVER THE LESS AFTER ABOUT THREE MONTHS THE FIRM I WORKED FOR REQUESTED ME TO GO TO NIGHT SCHOOL, AND ON THE LUNCH HOUR THAT PARTICULAR DAY WHILE WALKING HOME TO LUNCH ERNIE THOMAS PULLED UP AND GAVE ME A LIFT HOME, AS I LIVED ON HIS COAL-WHARF IN A HOUSE BELONGING TO HIM, AS MY FATHER WA HIS

The written life story of Charlie Foster before editing.

4

Stratford-upon-Avon

Stratford-upon-Avon's charm stretches from season to season and year to year, as visitors pour in from every corner of the globe, eager to catch a glimpse of the legend and magic of its most illustrious inhabitant. When I went along on a bright October Sunday recently, the town was as busy as on any holiday. However, aficionados of inland waterways have a second reason to visit this town of history and character, for it is a junction of canal and river, both of significance. Although, due to the difficulties of parking in this busy town, I shall tell you perhaps a better way of entering the town by foot. Half a mile out of Stratford along the A439 Warwick road, is a perfect little picnic-come-parking spot that sets the visitor right on the banks of the gently winding river Avon. After parking your car and lunching at one of the picnic tables, you can take a very pleasant stroll into town whilst watching others just mess about in boats. It's about fifteen minutes' walk.

An alternative route if you fancy a much longer walk takes in the olde worlde charm of the village of Wilmcote, plus the half-timbered building known as Mary Arden's house, and then a walk following the last sixteen locks of the Stratford Canal. Mary Arden's house, by the way, is reputed to be the home of Shakespeare's mother. This red-tiled collection of higgledy piggledy gables, like many of its genre, has settled and twisted itself to the shape of the landscape and is only a few hundred yards from the towpath. So, you could park nearby, enjoy the ambience of an imaginary seventeenth century, before advancing through to the nineteenth when the canal was born. Besides, entering the town via the canal has got to be the most enjoyable way, as it wriggles through the suburbs from the north-west, sneaking under roads and railway alike.

Certainly Stratford has seen some changes recently, including some external additions to the famous Royal Shakespeare Theatre, and there was a notable addition to the canal basin. But, I must admit that I was seriously disappointed with the new bridge at the tail of the river to basin lock. Five years ago, there was a very suitable footbridge, having a gentle curve to create extra strength, which

The River Avon just below the Royal Shakespeare Theatre.

carried the thousands of basin visitors from one side of the lock to the other. It was unpretentious but was perfectly harmonious with the canal and river scene. I have included a picture of it more of a statement of ill favour than anything else. Its glinting steel base and bars may very well have graced the interior of a modern factory, but not an important historical transition point for the canal and the River Avon.

Take away the Shakespeare connection and the town would still be a delightful one to visit, and I daresay that the locals would predominate in the scene rather than the eager Americans, lines of European students or camera-swinging Japanese tourists that fill the streets during summer months. In some respects the town reminds me a little of Stourport, another place where canal joins river. But today there is only one terminal basin left for the visitor to enjoy, where until 1926, there were two. Of course unlike Stourport, which grew up as a result of the canal, Stratford has flourished here since the twelfth century, and it has had a ford since Roman times. Right up until the eighteenth century the Avon provided a modicum of transport to the South West as well as powering the local mills, but for serious transport, the river had never been totally satisfactory, due to a lack of a towpath and the inconvenience of flash locks and low bridges. Meanwhile, during the seventeenth and eighteenth centuries, Birmingham, only 25 miles to the north, was growing rapidly. With its legendary 1,000 trades and growing wealth and status, it was impossible for the merchants of Stratford

Holy Trinity church, where Shakespeare is buried; from across the River Avon.

Bancroft Basin and statue of Lady Macbeth.

to ignore. They wanted a piece of Britain's growing action too. Money for the construction of the canal came from diverse pockets. One hundred and eighty-nine separate shareholders, from wealthy spinsters to yeomen and reverends, bought from one to ten shares. The majority of them were locals interested in opening up trade, but investors came from as far away as Banbury and London. All demonstrated their enthusiasm for the nation's new form of transport, and all hoped for a healthy financial return.

By 1792 there was a serious plan to take a canal from the Wednesbury coalfields through to Stratford, but in the end it was decided that the canal should join the Birmingham and Worcester Canal 5 miles south of Birmingham at Kings Norton Junction. After twenty-three years and £300,000, the Stratford-upon-Avon Canal was finally opened on 24 June 1816, one year after the W&B.

The new bridge at the tail of the lock.

The recently remodelled Royal Shakespeare Theatre.

Boat leaving the Colin P. Withers river lock. This is almost opposite Holy Trinity church.

Entering the basin from the River Avon.

Stratford's Bancroft canal basin.

Lots of visitors on a bright October Sunday in 2010.

Interior of Holy Trinity church, only five minutes' walk from the canal basin.

The grave of William Shakespeare. The slab set into the floor of the church reads 'Here lies William Shakespeare. Good frend for Jesus Sake Forbeare. To dig the Dust Encloased Heare. Bleste Be The Man That Spares Thes Stones, And Curst Be He That Moves My Bones.'

Shakespeare's birthplace; only five minutes' walk into the town from the basin.

One of the marvellous windows inside Holy Trinty church.

Today, only old black and white photographs can help to capture the essence of what Stratford was like during the canal-carrying era. In fact, it is probably as difficult to imagine what life was like along the canal and basins up to the First World War, as it is to conjure up Shakespeare's Stratford, so much has altered. For instance, during the seventeenth century, the half-timbered buildings with their off-white panels and protruding black timbers, were probably all panelled over in that century. Likewise, during the first half of the twentieth century, all of the warehouses and buildings that had been associated with the canal for over 100 years were demolished for modernisation. Hutchings' coal merchants was cleared to make way for the bus station; and Cox's timber yard, the brickworks, lime kilns and Flowers Brewery all suffered a similar fate. So only with an inward eye can we imagine the processions of coal boats supplying Stratford's gas works, and then the tar boats removing the by-products of that trade. And, as the coal came south from Birmingham, wheat and barley was emptied from farm carts into waiting boats ready to feed the hungry mouths in the Black Country.

After pottering around the basin for some time mulling over such things, I grabbed the missus's arm and we went to pay homage to Shakespeare with a visit to Holy Trinity church. This is only a five-minute walk past the Royal Shakespeare Theatre, following the road around to the left as you parallel the Avon, and you can't miss it. Inside you will see some wonderful stained-glass windows, marvellous carved pews and connected woodwork, and of course the grave of Stratford's most famous son.

5

The Story Of The World's Oldest Steam Engine

In the first quarter of the eighteenth century, crude atmospheric steam engines such as the one designed by Newcomen had limited success in pumping water out of mines. This engine, however, was highly inefficient and a number of inventive minds had been attracted to the prospects of producing a much more useful steam engine. James Watt was one of this number. He started to study the

Birmingham main line canal. The Soho foundry, where steam engine parts were made.

The Engine Arm, Smethwick, still much used as a safe mooring. The engine was housed at the end of this arm. Water from Rotton Park reservoir came along this arm, as did the re-circulated water from the bottom lock.

effects of steam in 1759, and in 1763 he was asked to try and get working a model of a Newcomen engine, belonging to Glasgow University.

In the Newcomen engine, steam entered a cylinder, underneath a piston. Then cold water was injected into the cylinder, causing rapid cooling of the steam and producing a great drop in pressure. Atmospheric pressure on the top of the large piston was then strong enough to drive the piston down on its stroke. The process then started again. Watt soon realised that the Newcomen was fundamentally flawed and there was much room for improvement. Watt, however, was employed on other matters – and steam engines were more of a fascinating distraction – and several years passed by. It was only after much thought and experimentation that he had an inventive brainwave. This was to enclose the piston and cylinder, and then add a separate device for cooling the steam. These two improvements increased the pressure within the cylinder and also prevented heat loss in the cylinder.

Engine Arm aqueduct.

While Watt was trying to solve the technical problems of applied steam power, canal building had commenced in the Midlands. On a technological point, it is worth noting that many of the problems that Watt encountered were due to the poor manufacture of cylinders; and that the iron master, John Wilkinson, had at that same time overcome these inaccuracies by using a boring machine that had been developed for making cannons for the European war.

When Brindley drew up his plans for the Birmingham Canal, he noted the problem caused by the high stretch of ground at Smethwick. He suggested that the canal could go around to the north, go under by means of a tunnel, or go over the top with the use of locks, plus a reservoir to supply the summit section with water. However, he also envisaged that it would be necessary for steam engines to re-circulate the water. This is in itself is an interesting point as it clearly demonstrates Brindley's knowledge of steam power and the possible application for canals.

The tunnel plan was abandoned when quicksand was found at the summit, so locks were built. The Birmingham Canal climbed via three locks on the West Bromwich side and then descended via six locks on the Smethwick side.

Smethwick bottom lock. Water was taken from the tail of this lock by a brick culvert to the engine.

Rotton Park reservoir, one of the main supplies for the Birmingham canals, both past and present.

Smethwick Summit and the Old Brindley Line.

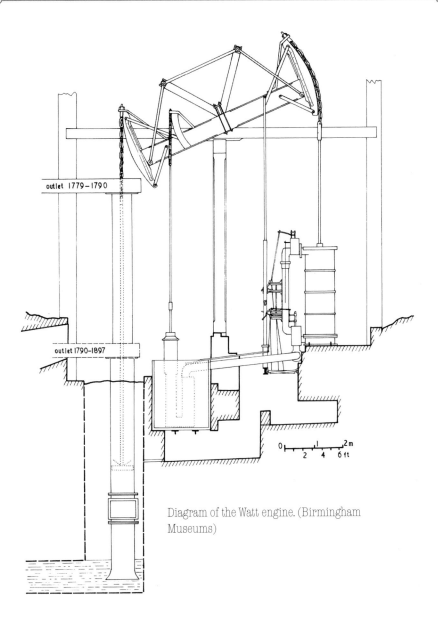

outlet 1779–1790

outlet 1790–1897

0   1   2 m
     2   4   6 ft

Diagram of the Watt engine. (Birmingham Museums)

Another set of three locks took the canal from Spon Lane down to the Wednesbury Canal. All this opened in 1769; and the whole of the Birmingham Canal through to the Staffordshire and Worcestershire Canal at Aldersley opened in 1772. Traffic increased quickly and the company realised the urgent need for water. A reservoir had been built at Smethwick, but due to constant leakage it was not a complete solution. In August 1776, the canal company sent their engineer, Samuel Bull, to see James Watt about the use of a steam engine to back-pump water lost down the locks.

Following discussions with Boulton and Watt about pumping engines, the Birmingham Canal Company ordered their first engine to be installed at Spon Lane, in West Bromwich, to back-pump water. That engine started work in April 1778, and a second was ordered for back-pumping up the Smethwick locks. The second engine was commissioned the following year. But even with two engines at work, it was still difficult to maintain useful water levels. During the 1780s, John Smeaton produced a detailed report on the water supply to this important transport route and in 1790 the company acted. Several

Birmingham Canal Navigations Ocker Hill depot, 1950s. The Watt engine was housed here for some years in the building in the background, and steamed on special occasions. Henry Ford offered a huge sum of money for the engine but was fortunately turned down.

The Watt engine at Millennium Point, Birmingham. It has been here since the transfer from the old Science Museum.

books report that it was Smeaton that oversaw the work, but according to a Mr Andrew, the records show that the lowering of the canal by excavating through the summit and thus eradicating the top six locks was conducted by their own superintendent, John Bough, and the engineer Samuel Bull. When this extensive work was completed, the Spon Lane engine was removed as unnecessary.

Because the Smethwick engine was not far from Boulton and Watt's factory, Watt himself was able to visit the engine and conduct a number of experiments. From these experiments he was able to make further technical advances to the operation and hence the efficiency of this and later engines. Thus the Smethwick engine played an important role in the development of Watt's engine. The engine was connected to the canal by means of an underground brick culvert that went from the tail end of the Smethwick bottom lock, along to the engine that was sited a hundred yards away at the corner of Rolfe Street and Bridge Street.

Industrial and urban development around the Birmingham Canal continued during the final decades of the eighteenth century, thus contributing to its use. As a consequence of the growing number of boats on the system, it became apparent that improvements to the route were needed. In 1824, Thomas Telford was engaged to survey the whole route and report his ideas for improvements. There were three main aims; to provide a wider and straighter line, to improve the water supply and to bypass the Smethwick locks, which were by then causing some delay. These grand improvements were to take six years, and they included a new motorway style canal having twin towpaths, the cutting off of several meandering loops, the construction of the Rotton Park reservoir and the building of new bridges and aqueducts, one of which included the Engine Arm aqueduct. This gothic-styled aqueduct carried the feed from the Rotton Park reservoir and from the two steam engines across the new line and onto the old line just above the Smethwick locks.

After the Engine Arm aqueduct and the navigable feeder canal were constructed, there came to be three canals lying side by side – a unique feature to Birmingham. The new reservoir at Edgbaston was truly enormous. With a length of just over half a mile, and a width of a third of a mile, the reservoir held 13,000 gallons of water in its locks. And with its surface 22ft higher than the summit canal, the water could be delivered by gravity along the Engine Arm branch.

Over the years, various canal companies, including the Birmingham Company, went on to purchase more of the Boulton and Watt steam engines and distribute

The rocking beam, or top of the Watt engine.

The huge cast-iron cylinder containing the piston for the engine.

them throughout the growing canal network. Thus, through utilising reservoirs with their feeders, with the addition of strategically placed steam engines, the Birmingham Company solved its water supply problems. (Three engines went to the Ocker Hill site in 1784, 1791 and 1803.) In 1803, Boulton and Watt overhauled the Smethwick engine and fitted a larger cylinder, then a second engine was installed alongside it two years later. The Smethwick engine continued to pump water up the Smethwick locks for 112 years until 1891. A few years later, the second engine was scrapped, and the original went for safe-keeping to the BCN depot at Ocker Hill. The day of large steam beam engines had come to an end and they were gradually replaced by second generation steam engines that operated on higher steam pressures and were more powerful.

From 1898, the engine lived in its own purpose-built house at Ocker Hilland was treated as a curiosity. It was only steamed on special occasions or when interested parties wanted to view the workings of this most fascinating piece of Britain's industrial heritage. For the purpose of steaming the engine, a portable boiler was placed in a boat and moved to the basin next to the building in which it was stationed. The engine did not require enormous pressure to get it going. Probably the most important visitor was the famous US car manufacturer – Henry Ford. He came to Britain in 1928 in order to secure exhibits for the museum in Detroit.

Now imagine that you own a priceless object, and it's the only one in the world. Then someone comes along and offers you an unlimited amount of money for that item. What would you do? Well that's what happened when Henry Ford visited Ocker Hill that year. The Watt engine would, of course, have been a most impressive addition for his museum, and he offered the BCN a blank cheque to purchase it. Fortunately he was turned down and the Watt engine stayed where it was.

Then in 1959, after almost seventy years, it became apparent that great changes were afoot for the canal system. Britain's waterway operations had by then been nationalised, and plans had been made to close the Ocker Hill depot and move its operations to a new depot in Bradley on the Wednesbury Oak Loop. What would happen to the Watt engine? Fortunately, in 1951, buildings had been secured to house the Birmingham Museum of Science and Industry at Newhall Street, Birmingham – situated right next to the Farmer's Bridge flight of locks. And preparations were made to have it installed there in 1959. The engine was first steamed at that site in 1979.

For forty years, the Watt engine was housed in the Engineering Hall and for twenty years steamed on regular occasions for the entertainment and education of visitors. Then at the turn of the century a totally new and innovative building was constructed to take over the work of the old Museum of Science and Industry, and the Watt engine had its final move to Thinktank at Millennium Point IN Birmingham – where you can go and view it in action today.

My thanks go to Birmingham Science Museum at Millennium Point, and Mr Jim Andrew for their able assistance in the making of this article.

6

The Stourbridge Canal and the Glass Industry

A walk down the Stourbridge locks is a very satisfying way of passing an hour or two, but probably the most intriguing feature on that walk is the sight of the Redhouse Cone belonging to Stuart Crystal. I realised that my knowledge of the glass trade was minimal, so I decided to do some research and discovered a fascinating history. The story of the glass industry in Stourbridge is one of

The bottle kiln belonging to Stuart Crystal, now part of the museum.

The Bonded warehouse, Stourbridge, where taxable items were locked away. Glass was heavily taxed at one time.

The glass kiln, early twentieth century.

A glassmaker at work. The gathered glass at the end of the iron is being rolled on the long arms of the glassmaker's chair.

Modern glassworker at his bench. The principles have stayed pretty much the same although the centuries.

religious persecution, hard-sweated toil, child labour, secret skills and recipes and, of course, the utilisation of the canal system. But how did glassmaking come to the heart of the Midlands in the first place?

Glassmaking, in all its primitive forms, goes back several thousand years, but it was only in the first century BC that glass vessels as we know them made their appearance. It was then that the glassmakers discovered that molten glass could be blown into a variety of shapes, and the use of the blowing iron became a most important technique. During the Roman Empire, glassmaking depended entirely on the skills, knowledge and closely guarded secrets of individual craftsmen.

Over hundreds of years that knowledge was passed on from masters to their apprentices, and glassmaking gradually spread throughout Europe. There were two methods of producing flat glass, and both involved blowing a bubble into the glass. In the 'crown' method, the glassmaker blew a large bubble of glass, which he then spun rapidly while still very hot and soft. Centrifugal force produced a disc of glass, which was later cut into panes of different sizes. In the cylinder method,

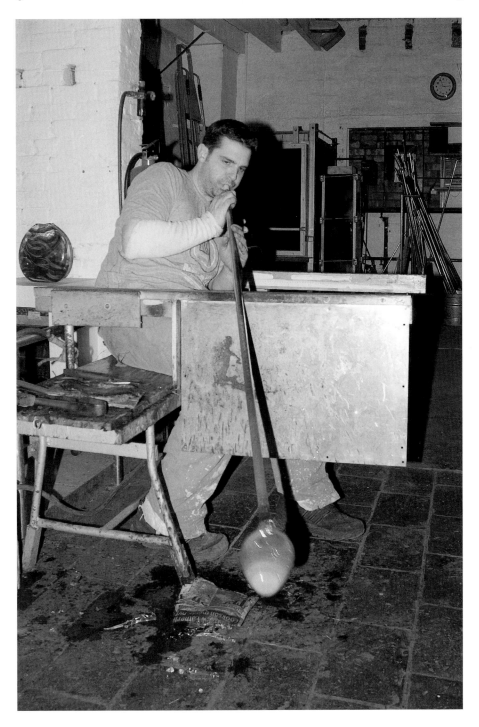

Blowing the 'gather'.

Broadfield House glass museum, Stourbridge.

the glassmaker blew a bubble, which he elongated by swinging the iron in a pit, thus producing a cylinder of glass closed at both ends. The ends were then cut off and the cylinder cut lengthwise; the glass was then re-heated and opened out into a flat sheet.

England has long been an attractive place for asylum seekers, and during the sixteenth century certain religious groups on the continent, who were being persecuted for their faith, decided that England was the best place for them to continue their trade and bring up their families. They then spent the second half of that century putting down roots in different parts of the country. Annanias de Hennezel, his brother Israel and his mother, who had owned a glassworks in Lorraine, first settled in the Forest of Dean and later Newcastle, but they moved to the Stourbridge area when wood for fuel became scarce, and experiments in the Dudley area had proved successful using coal. Stourbridge had many of the raw ingredients needed for the manufacture of glass, including clay (for the pots), coal and sand. Annanias and his son Joshua commenced production on a site unknown, while Paul Tyzack rented a field near the river Stour. The Stour was presumably used for either transport or power, but the small size of that river was never going to prove truly successful. The main work on the Stour was done between 1665 and 1667 by Andrew Yarranton, who built twelve locks between Stourbridge and Kidderminster to take 16-ton craft, transporting mainly coal, but work stopped due to a funding shortage.

The transport of coal was still a motivating force 100 years later, but by then there were the plans and the capital to build a Stourbridge and a Dudley canal. A capital of £30,000 was authorised, and the leading promoters were Lords Dudley and Ward (who owned most of the land and thus the mineral rights for the area). Lord Dudley wanted to sell his coal, but amongst the promoters of the canal schemes were several glassmakers, and it was apparent that their requirements had influenced the route chosen, because many of them ended up with their premises close to or right next to the towpath. Francis Homfray of Wollaston Hall, an ironmaster, was made treasurer, and Thomas Dadford junior was engineer at £120 per annum, with James Green as assistant. They made their start on the Stour Aqueduct, and the line was open to a junction at Stourton 3¼ miles away on the Staffordshire and Worcestershire Canal, and thus to the Severn at Stourport by December of 1779.

Advertisement for Stevens and Williams glass products.

Looking down the Stourbridge 'sixteen' towards the cone; Dadford's shed is in the middle ground.

For the Dudley Canal, Abiathar Hawkes, glassmaker of Dudley, was appointed treasurer, with Thomas Dadford senior as engineer and surveyor. By 1796 the canal was carrying 100,000 tons per year, and much of that tonnage was coal, sand and clay to the various glassworks, and then finished products down to Stourport, where they were transhipped to Bristol for national and international distribution.

Looking up the Stourbridge locks, with the delightful Samson and Lion pub behind.

GLASS CONES

The brick-built cone, towering 100ft above the landscape, performed a dual function. Ultimately the structure is a chimney, designed to create great flows of air through the central furnace and thus maintain the high temperatures required for the melting of glass, but opened out at the base, it also provided the area for the glassmakers to work in. Inside, the atmosphere was hot, smoky and full of noise as the teams of men and boys worked day and night. Until the Second World War, glasshouses like Stuart's operated twenty-four hours a day. The temperatures in front of the furnace were enormous, and the glare from the molten glass caused eye-strain. Manipulating large gathers of glass at the end of the iron required great physical strength, and there was a continual risk of being badly burned. During the nineteenth century, child labour was used in the glass trade like any other industry, and boys were used for the menial tasks such as cleaning tools, fetching and carrying articles or the beer that the men drank to stop them dehydrating.

Just a small sample of the beautiful glassware produced in Stourbridge.

THE GLASS TRADE TODAY

During the nineteenth century, many glass cones graced the landscape around Stourbridge, but today only the Redhouse Cone remains as an educational facility and museum. The Dial glassworks still stands on the side of the Stourbridge Canal, but the top of its cone was taken off in the early part of the twentieth century. The company was taken over by Plowden and Thompson who, as glass specialists, produce a wide range of products that include capillary tubing, coloured glasses, and components for the medical, electronic and engineering industries. Just a short distance away from the Redhouse Cone is the Broadfield House Glass Museum, with its world-famous collections of glass.

So if you are thinking of taking a stroll down the Stourbridge locks, why not include the museum and cone on your list of places to visit?

7

Water Management

Probably the most important job for any waterway agency is the management of its water. Take away the water and all we are left with is a dry, useless ditch. I believe that I speak for the majority of us when I say that we generally take our water supplies for granted. We lock up, we lock down, ten minutes fly by as 50,000 or so gallons rush past the paddles in the most fascinating fashion, and another lockfull of water is gone and on its way to the sea. Therefore, to get a

Hatton locks, Warwick, where SCADA is installed at the top and bottom of the flight.

British Waterways headquarters at Hatton, where the Water Management team has been based since 2004.

better understanding of how our water is managed, I went along to see British Waterways Hydrology Manager at Warwick, Adam Comerford. But first let us take a look at how they did it in the past.

In the old days, a canal operative, possibly a lengthsman, would simply drop a rod or stick into a pound to see how much water there was available, just like you test the oil in your car. But today, in our computer-operated society, with possibly more boating activity than ever before, we need to be a bit more sophisticated with our use of this precious commodity. So it will be interesting to contrast the old with the new methods. When the canals were first built, engineers naturally included reservoirs in the design and construction of a waterway. Land was purchased, navvies were hired, and the reservoir was placed as high as possible in relation to the summit pound. And as boats went off through the locks, the summit pound was topped up via gravity to keep the levels constant. Nevertheless, engineers like Brindley realised that reservoirs alone, fed by streams, would not be enough, and during the construction of the early Birmingham Canal, he approached Messrs Boulton and Watt with regard to the purchasing of steam engines to recirculate water. Watt's first pumping engines were built around 1776 – just in time for the fledgling canals – and the first two were ordered in 1777 and 1778, and fitted to the Spon Lane (West Bromwich) and Smethwick locks; and back-pumping made began.

Of course we still back-pump today, but not by the magnificent rocking splendour of the enormous clanking and hissing steam engines of James Watt's day.

Monitoring sensor cover with a galvanised box at the top of the Hatton flight.

Bumble Hole, Netherton, on the Dudley No. 2 Canal; a familiar sight to many boaters. The building that once housed the steam pumping engine, emptying the mines and simultaneously topping up the canal, sits on the distant hillside.

Nevertheless, a few of those wonderful iconic structures survive to grace our modern landscape, and include the recently restored BCN'S headquarters in Oldbury, and the Crofton pumping station on the Kennet and Avon Canal (still steamed on special open days).

RIVERS, STREAMS, MINE DRAINAGE AND RUN-OFF

Minor rivers and streams were often diverted by the early canal companies as a useful source of water – much to the chagrin of local mill and industry owners. When Thomas Telford built the Llangollen Canal for instance, he very cleverly tapped into the River Dee by designing the Horseshoe Falls some 2 miles beyond Llangollen. And by drawing off 6,000,000 gallons a day, he secured sufficient water for the canal and a source of water at Hurlston reservoir for a large part of Cheshire. A second source of water in industrial areas came from the draining of coal mines, and Cobb's engine house at Netherton is a classic example of that. As J.M. Pearson put it succinctly in his guidebook to the Stourport Ring, the engine kept the mines dry and the cut wet. That pumping station was erected in 1831 to clear water from the underground shafts of the Windmill End coal mines.

Water quality is continually tested on the Llangallen Canal. Here samples are being taken to be tested at the lab for contamination.

This wonderful building sitting at the top of Oldbury locks was also an important back-pumping station. It has now been revitalised as the home of the BCN Society.

The M5 overhead section in West Bromwich can supply 10 million gallons of water per day into the canal below.

Those mines eventually went down as far as 522ft, and that engine, pumping steadily at eight strokes per minute, emptied some 367,000 gallons each day into the Dudley Canal.

Concerns about the weather are all part and parcel of being British, yet our rainy days are so important. And when it comes to calculating run-off, you may be surprised how much water enters the canal from roads and roofs. Our canal network serves as an extremely valuable function as routes for land and storm-water drainage, and on the BCN alone there are around 800 recorded drain connections controlling some 850 million gallons daily during rainy weather. The overhead section of the M5 alone will contribute 10 million gallons per day on a wet day into the massive weir built near Spon Lane locks. Interestingly, during the 1960s, when many authorities were considering shutting their respective canals down, they realised that they would find it extremely difficult and costly to find a suitable alternative to storm drainage. On Merseyside, three schemes were examined for handling storm water should the canal be eliminated from

The attractive Engine Arm aqueduct serves as a feeder from Rotten Park onto the Brindley Line at Smethwick.

the equation. The cost of these ranged from £310,000 per mile for a fully piped system, to £230,000 per mile for a combination of pumping stations, pipes and open ponds. Calculations showed that for the BCN alone, the overall capital cost of replacement would have been in the region of £20 million, and that didn't include the following yearly maintenance figures. Canal engineers and water authorities have therefore ended up with a variety of means of obtaining and managing their water supplies; rainfall from rivers and streams into reservoirs, along with back-pumping, operation of sluices, and general storm run-off. Certainly Tom Rolt and Alan Aikman played a huge part in saving the canal system, but the unglamorous other reason is that our canals were saved to some degree by their usefulness as a drain.

To cope with the enormous demands for water, at the end of the 1990s, British Waterways started to fit an electronic, computer-controlled monitoring system called SCADA. The acronym stands for Supervisory Control and Data Acquisition. Yes it sounds like a line from Star Trek, but SCADA is an essential piece of modern kit if waterway operators are to know where their water is, where it is coming from, where it is going, and, most importantly, will they have enough of the for the future? The SCADA scheme commenced on the canals of the north-east, including the Aire and Calder River and the canal system in Yorkshire, and over the following years came to rapidly encompass all of the waterways of Scotland, England and Wales. In the early years there was a Water Management Team stationed in Leeds and Watford, but more recently (2004) both relocated to the central British Waterways headquarters at Hatton, Warwick. Of course not every lock and pound is covered by SCADA, nor needs to be, but 600 monitoring sites stationed at selected points across the system feed enough information into the central computer for water engineers to get a rapid picture of the water situation and manage it effectively. There are two essential types of measuring devices: the first is a pressure transducer, which measures the pressure of water; and the second is a stilling well, which is a tube-like arrangement about 200mm across containing a float that responds to changing water levels. As the float moves up and down within the tube it controls a sensitive electronic device which then sends signals to SCADA via telephone lines, or more lately by 3G wireless systems. The devices can then automatically control electronic pumps or simply be read on a laptop anywhere. These carefully engineered instruments are made for any organisation concerned with the management of water supplies by a variety of manufacturers such as Mitsubishi and Dynamic Logic.

THE BRADLEY DEPOT

The Bradley Depot of Bilston stands at the end of what remains of the Bradley Loop (BCN). Historically this was the site of 'Iron Mad' Wilkinson's Ironworks, but in the 1950s it was developed as an important depot for British Waterways, following the closure of the much larger depot at Ocker Hill. It is still an essential place for the manufacture of lock gates, but of equal importance is the fact that many millions of gallons of groundwater are pumped up and into the Wolverhampton level from this location. The station is very much a combination and contrast of the old and the new. The building looks like any misused one-storey Victorian building, but inside are the most up-to-date electrical pumps and computer-monitoring technologies, and, connected to SCADA, it enables engineers anywhere in the country to look at their monitor and instantly view the state of any of the levels on the BCN.

A couple of years ago the site manager, Mark Ashlee, was kind enough to show me what went on in the dark bowels of that useful building. After descending a long flight of metal stairs, Mark flicked on a fluorescent light and there in front of us were three powerful electrical motors attached to the heads of the main risers; or in other words, a lot of big pipework. All of the water at this point is drawn from the water table and old mine shafts at a depth of around 36 metres, and you wouldn't want to fall down the hole next to those pumps. The pumps then feed all of the groundwater into the Bradley arm only yards away. A monitor on the wall showed that at that precise moment, 322 litres per second was flowing into the Wolverhampton level.

When an operator logs on to the SCADA site, he sees a map of the country before him, and by zooming in, can view increasing amounts of information about the management of a specific area. For instance, at Hatton a monitoring device sits happily at the top and bottom of the lock flight. From the 1990s onward, there was a growing investment in brand new back-pumping systems. These are often stationed out of sight below ground along lock flights, or sited in a dedicated brick structure. Sometimes the pumps lift water back through just one lock, or in other cases underground pipework re-circulates water from the bottom of a lock flight to the top. The SCADA units at the top then shut off the pumps, thus saving energy and excess water from simply running through the by-washes.

At this point it IS worth mentioning how much usage we get out of our locks, and it all depends on where they are sited. For instance, some locks may only operate a few dozen times a year – say on the backwaters of the BCN. But on very busy sections of our waterways, say on the Llangollen, or central sections of

Bradley pumping station. Three pump heads pour groundwater into one outlet pipe.

the Grand Union at Marston Doles, a lock may empty and fill over 10,000 times per year. Let us say, for example, that a lock contains, in round figures, 50,000 gallons of water; times this by 10,000, and we see that 500,000,000 gallons of water flow through *one* lock every year. This is a serious amount of water, and hard work on the lock. Multiply this by the amount of lockages in just one year and the figures for water flow are almost astronomic. To ensure levels stay static, back-pumping alone costs around £800,000 per year in electricity, without consideration for installation or maintenance costs. And just to give a hint at the figures, we see there are about 1,600 locks in our system, supplied by ninety-five reservoirs, constantly monitored by 130 SCADA installations. Reservoirs are a very important part of the picture, though British Waterways is not currently building any more due to the massive cost.

Graphs and charts are also exceedingly useful to the water engineer and modeller. The SCADA system includes graphs of the holding power of all of our reservoirs, showing the percentage of their capacity. Rotten Park reservoir on the BCN for instance, completed in 1828, contains on average 1,457,810 cubic metres of water. This flows under gravity via the Rotten Park loop and over the Engine Arm aqueduct into the Old Brindley Line at Smethwick. The Leeds and Liverpool Canal, much further north, receives some of its water from the Winterburn reservoir (1891) and contains a similar amount at 1,234,790 cubic metres. In the Midlands during 2009 there were concerns regarding the reservoir

Meter recording the pumping rate of 320 litres per minute into the Bradley Loop.

at Chasewater – a major contributor to the BCN, where a 200-year-old dam was in danger of collapse. This vital reservoir has since been drained and will soon be up and running again at a cost of around £3 million, a point that vividly demonstrates the cost of keeping a 200-year-old system going. And as we all recognise, weather patterns change; 1934 and 1959 were, for example, very dry years, and helped to drain the reservoirs and pounds. Recent developments point to global warming, but as yet there seems to be no obvious identifiable trends; nevertheless 2010 was a truly dry year, with some months having as little as 12 per cent of their usual rainfall. All these factors have an effect on the water that is available throughout the entire system.

On the positive side, early canal companies, British Waterways and no doubt its successor, the Waterways Trust, have sold, and will continue to sell, water to a variety of customers. Historically, much water was sold to coal-fired electricity generators. These have generally disappeared, though many industries and agricultural concerns continue to purchase water. New customers include the ultra-modern Data Warehouses; places that are jam-packed with hot computers which all need cooling. So, canal water is piped to the companies' heat exchangers, heat is transferred to the water, computers are cooled, and the water is then piped back to the canal a few degrees warmer. It's all about looking for new business opportunities.

One of the new challenges for water usage is the burgeoning use of leisure craft, and the question that has been asked recently is – will the system become too congested? Tie this in with the possibilities of climate change and we have a recipe for water shortage. Commentators have said more than once that there are now more boats on the system than there were in the days of canal carrying. That may well be true, but the pattern of water usage is very different. In the old days, canal companies worked their boats fifty-two weeks a year, and the usage was steady and regular. But today there are marked peaks and troughs. The peaks include the summer months when most people take their holidays, or in the spring and autumn breaks, when the kids are off school. Unfortunately for water supplies, this increased usage happens to coincide with the driest months.

SCADA sensing point on the Bradley Loop.

Wall displays showing various water levels at Bradley loop.

Today, we are experiencing the excitement of seeing the opening of canals old and new. The Droitwich Canal came online during the summer of 2011, while other projects are, at the time of writing, under way. This all adds up to a greater demand for water that has to be managed by the water engineers, who have to use all of the data at their disposal to predict what the future demands may be. Just think how foolish it would be to open a new canal, only to discover that there wasn't enough water to run it properly?

If you are of a certain age, you may fondly recall the summer of 1976, and boy what a summer that was; blue skies and hot days that never seemed to end. Certainly there was a downside to all that fun, and it included the drying up of many rivers and streams, including problems for the canal system. Nowadays, canal engineers take 1976 as a kind of benchmark and ask themselves – could we operate successfully if we had another summer like 1976? Added to this comes new EU legislation regarding licences to extract water, water quality, and associated concerns about the environment.

So, we can sum up by concluding that our canal system is an entirely artificial one, nothing like the streams, rivers and lakes of nature that find their own balance; that SCADA, with access to huge amounts of meteorological data, are marvellous assets to waterway operators; and that you and I now have a deeper,

Outlet flow at Bradley loop.

Lower Bittell reservoir next to the Worcester and Birmingham canal. This was built to compensate local water users after construction of the canal. The Upper reservoir (not shown) feeds the waterway (capacity 31,190 cubic metres of water).

An empty Chasewater reservoir in 2011, with the dam being repaired.

Adam Comerford, head of the hydrology team at Hatton.

New canals mean more water. This is the opening of the Droitwich canals in July 2011.

more appreciative view of what our modern waterway engineers have to do year in and year out to keep those water levels just where we like them.

8

Jack Haddock's World of the Walsall Canals

Jack Haddock, now a sprightly eighty-something, did not set out to catalogue the final days of the working boat around Walsall, but that is what happened from the 1930s through to the 1970s. Jack still rides his bicycle to the Walsall History Centre most weeks, and his contribution to the film data stored at that location in Essex Street is enormous. Jack's first love was steam trains – well no one's perfect – but the lens of his camera was soon pointed at all kinds of transportation. Towards the end of the Second World War, it dawned on him that

Ken Keay's tug the *Dart* towing 'ampton' boats at Norton Canes, Cannock extension canal, 1947.

Ernie Thomas's boat *Enterprise* towing boats from Holly Bank to Birchills for breaking. This was the end of the line for many working boats on the BCN.

A view of the old Walsall town arm during the 1970s.

the industrial world of horse-drawn boats and belching smoke stacks was fast disappearing. Jack describes one of his earliest memories:

> My first recollections of Walsall were of a view from the balcony of a Corporation tramcar, as it rose over the steep hump of a narrow canal bridge en route to Bloxwich. As you approached the bridge, there was the majestic sight of Pratt's Flour Mill with its imposing height and numerous small windows covered in flour dust. Down below on the canal I saw a number of finely painted narrowboats unloading sacks of wheat. Opposite the mill was a small turnover bridge leading to Peter Keay and Sons boat dock.

A continual relay of horse-drawn boats visited Pratt's Mill but in the late 1930s tugs began to appear, towing a butty each. The horse would be accommodated at Keay's at the charge of sixpence per night. Prior to the Second World War, Pratt's Mill was taken over by Price's bread, which worked at full capacity during the desperate days of the war. One nightly ritual was the fitting of stop planks under the bridge by the local Civil Defence force – just in case the canal happened to be bombed by the Luftwaffe. Work rapidly dropped off after the war, and the mill's working life came to an abrupt end with a disastrous fire in 1952. Today and as with many stretches of canal, this place is now devoid of character.

Birchills' power station, and the trial of the first Truman Boat. H.F. Truman is an enterprise to get young people engaged with the waterways. Their first boat was built by Ken Keay at his boat dock, off Carl Street, Walsall.

One of the last coal transports from Birchills to Oldbury. Caggy Steven's boat and horse are seen here.

One of the early Rally's at Walsall around 1984. (K. Hodgkins)

Ken Keay and Caggy Stevens had one of the last canal contracts to deliver pipes for the distribution of natural gas during the early 1970s.

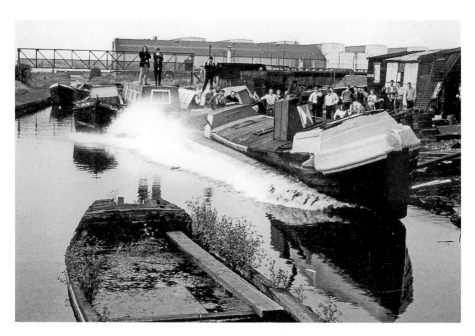

Many will be familiar today with Thomas Clayton's boat *Gifford* as it travels around the canals. This is the re-launch of the boat in 1976 at Ken Keay's boatyard after much repair work.

Walsall bottom lock, 1970s. The area has seen much redevelopment over the years.

The mid-1930s was a period stricken with unemployment, so government improvement schemes included the renewal of Pratt's Mill Bridge. The new Pratt's Mill Bridge was one of a number that were widened for burgeoning road transport. On the west side of the bridge were two coal wharves belonging to H.S. Thomas, and Bunch & Co. respectively; both owned their own narrowboats and also operated horse-drawn drays for home delivery.

Jack Haddock's first camera was a Kodak box type, and then later a slightly better Zeiss Nettar which cost £20 – a lot of money in 1954 – before moving on to a 35mm Pentax Spotmatic. I continued to photograph the changes happening in the Walsall area. The old boat companies were shutting one by one after the Second World War, but Jimmy Yates carried on in Lime Lane Pelsall for some years, as did Ken Keay, who as late as 1968 built a boat for H.F. Truman, and still operates boats today for young people. One of the great canal characters of the past was Ernie Thomas, who ran a large boat company and lived next to Walsall locks, just above Walsall Flour Mill. Nevertheless, the day of the working boat had come to its natural end on the BCN and Thomas had the contract to scrap many of them. I recall in 1934 that a flying circus came to town and Ernie treated his boatmen to a flight for 5s each – ah … them was the days.

My thanks to Walsall History Centre and to Jack Haddock for preparing this article.

9

Walking the Severn Way

THE WELSH HILLS

Long-distance walking paths have increased in number and popularity over the last twenty years or so. Included in that ever-growing list is the footpath that generally follows the course of the River Severn; I say generally because, at the start of the walk, it is impossible to follow the fledgling river faithfully and the recognised path takes a few detours. Nevertheless, now can you deepen your acquaintance with this fascinating and beautiful river, to discover a little of its history, and watch it grow from a trickle to a watery highway.

Information board and picnic site at the official start of the Severn Way. The river is only five minutes' walk through the woods.

Baby coal tits are plentiful in the forest.

The 'Way' itself has developed as a joint project by the six local authorities, through which this wonderful winding river passes on its 210-mile course from its source at Plynlimon (near Llanidloes in central Wales) through to Bristol. Starting in the boggy Welsh hills, no more than 20 miles from the coast, the river runs north-east to Shrewsbury, passing the ancient Breidden Hills, before performing a great curve on to English soil, then running south towards the grand old ports of Tewksbury and Gloucester. The official walker's guidebook – a copy of which I encourage you to obtain – will take you all the way from a benign trickle in the Welsh hills to the wide estuary.

Certainly there are many ways to cover the ground. My intention was to carry everything with me in a rucksack – tent, clothing, food etc., and walk or use the country buses. And then either find a camping site or maybe a B&B if possible. You may of course wish to do the journey in a completely different way.

After carefully studying the well-drawn maps and text of the guidebook, I discovered that the first 40 miles or so only occasionally follow the actual river, due to the nature of the rocky and wooded terrain. The 'Way' utilises bridle paths and minor roads to accomplish this section for some miles, and then uses the route of the Montgomery Canal from Newtown to Pool Quay. So, I opted to take a look at the official start and then make a real start of walking at Pool Quay, as I had walked the Montgomery previously.

The start of the River Severn is 7 miles out of the Welsh town of Llanidloes, and is complete with car park, picnic site and rustic information board. The true

St Peter's church, Melverley. The early Saxon church was destroyed by Owain Glyndwr in 1401. This replacement was completed by 1406. A rare example of a timber, wattle and daub church, with all its original oak beams fixed with wooden pegs.

Himalayan Balsam has overtaken much of the river's banks.

source is still 2 miles away, lost in the dripping bogs of upland peat and moss. By the time it arrives at the picnic site, the river is already a tumbling torrent, tearing its way through the densely wooded Hafren Forest. At this point, the cool crystal water rushes noisily down small rocky falls and cascades. Before heading off to Pool Quay, I spent an hour or so observing this infant flood as it twisted and turned to follow the irregular landscape. The forest is extremely dense in places, with a mixture of trees and foliage, while blue, great and coal tits flit and call through the overreaching canopy of leaves.

I got a lift to Pool Quay, by which time the day was getting along, and it seemed rather late to start walking, however it was about time that I shouldered my thirty-pound pack and got on with the job. The Severn comes within a few hundred yards of the A483 at Pool Quay, so that is where I got going.

POOL QUAY

Two hundred years ago, Pool Quay was a small Severn-side settlement and was the effective terminus of the navigation at that time. But even then, the carriage of goods in small vessels was only possible during winter months, or if the water was unseasonably high. At Pool Quay, the river and the Montgomery Canal are only a few hundred yards apart, and will run parallel for some miles, both lying either side of the busy A483 that runs between Welshpool and Oswestry. I strolled across a scrubby undulating field and down to the now sluggish channel of the waterway.

The Breidden Hills.

At this point a long embankment about a metre high also runs parallel with the river, and here I made my first error of judgement. For some miles, the more well-trodden Offa's Dyke long-distance path coincides with the Severn Way, and I quickly came across two well-laden walkers in that first meadow – though going the opposite way. The 3ft-high embankment wasn't part of Offa's Dyke though, but part of the much more recent flood barrier scheme, built to control the river's advancement. Bird watching is an excellent way to add to the walking experience, and you may be lucky enough to catch sight of a Kingfisher along the riverbanks. Jays, though generally very shy birds and not easy to photograph, do seem to be increasing in numbers, and I spotted one in a tree.

Offa's Dyke, was and in some places still is, a substantial mound, built for Offa, the king of ancient Mercia, between AD 757 and AD 796. It was designed and constructed as a kind of border to separate two neighbouring kingdoms. Sometimes you hear it referred to as a barrier, but no mound of dirt a few metres high is ever going to be a barrier to human incursions. More recently the Dyke has been described as the longest archaeological monument in Britain – it stretches from Prestatyn on the north Welsh coast, with few breaks – to Chepstow in the south. And it's only when you consider the manpower required to undertake this kind of construction that you get a glimpse into the muscle power and the time that was required for this massive, prestigious project. Offa must have been a powerful guy in his world!

I quickly dropped into the meditative state of the solitary walker. Under blue skies and light fluffy clouds I followed the banks of the Severn, heading slowly but irrevocably towards the village of Llandrinio. Looming in front of me were the massive green forms of the Breidden Hills – not to be confused with Bredon Hill, which of course is many miles away. By six o'clock I had had enough of walking and found a secretive location to erect my small green tent. It was near a sharp bend of the river and at a place where I was unlikely to be disturbed. I am no great fan of rough camping but there was neither an official campsite or B&B for many miles, so it was the only option I had. My evening meal was a banana and pasty, but the greatest delight of the day was the sunset that began at about eight.

Over to the west, the rapidly descending sun was transforming little slips of cloud into gold and silver ribbons, while above the eastern horizon the sky was all soft blues and greys. Beneath them, the low distant hills were losing their earlier vivid hues to turn to blue/grey tones. A short distance away, the Breidden Hills rose almost precipitously out of an otherwise flat landscape, looking a little like the silhouette of a family of gargantuan camels at rest. Long lines of clouds spattered the sky as though an invisible steam train had earlier crossed the heavens, leaving a purple puffed trail in its wake. Crouched on the grass as the shadows lengthened, I watched a glowing golden ball sink into the soft horizon, marking the finis, of yet another twenty-four hours. I was about to spend the night with only the flimsiest of cloths between me and those great skies.

The jay. A beautiful bird, but one that shuns the company of people.

LLANDRINIO TO IRONBRIDGE

The Breidden Hills were only 2 miles south of my camping position, while Shrewsbury was roughly 10 miles to the east. The next morning I poked my head cautiously out of the tent flap to discover the source of unusual grinding noises. In front of me were six sheep in a semi-circle, munching grass in the noisiest manner and eyeing me with a look of disdain that only sheep do so well. Only yards away was a sharp bend in the river as it runs towards the village of Crew Green. Overhead was the palest of blue skies with a smattering of creamy chiffon clouds. I packed up my gear, making sure that the only evidence of my one night's residence was bent grass stalks. I threw the pack on my back and strode off in the direction of Crew Green, with the meandering Severn curling away to the left.

I joined the B4393 at Crew Green for a few hundred yards before turning left and crossing the river towards the tiny old village of Melverley, one mile distant. As you cross the river, you can see the point some yards away where the river Vyrnwy joins and swells the Severn. At this juncture I was particularly looking forward to seeing the half-timbered St Peter's church, for which the guidebook had whetted my appetite. At first glance, St. Peter's resembles a well-constructed timber barn of very modest proportions. I paced around its external walls, this giving me the rough dimensions of only 15 yards by 8 yards. Meanwhile, two very elderly gentlemen were attempting to bring some kind of order to the church garden by hacking away at the perimeter hedges. This delightful rural gem of a half-timbered church was amazingly – in this age of high security – unlocked; so I lifted the latch and went in. The interior was dimly lit, exuded a mild musty smell, and had a tangible quietness that only religious buildings manifest.

This inner space had the essence of a small sixteenth-century house or barn, but was equipped with the trappings of a place of worship, two rows of pews, a Saxon font, a lectern and stained-glass window at the far end. Above my head was the tiniest of galleries that more resembled a hayloft. In the corner, I climbed the dark stained, roughly hewn rickety oak steps, where no doubt hundreds of feet had trodden before me, to gain access to where the higher strata of the local society had sung praises and said their prayers. It was impossible not to sense the echoes of those past generations that now lay sleeping in the diminutive graveyard outside. My silent meditation was then interrupted by a small mouse that ran across the orange tiles and red aisle carpet below. Returning to the garden, I took a photograph of the magnificent view across the gravestones towards the Breiddens, while robins twittered in the bushes. It was then time to head off along narrow country lanes towards Wilcott Marsh and Shrawardine, about 5 miles away. The Severn, now a much greater river due to the addition of the

Acorn symbols mark the way across a stile near Pool Quay, just north of Welshpool.

Vyrnwy, looped away to the right. A passing farmer told me that he grew sugar beet, potatoes and wheat in the adjacent fields.

Two miles beyond Shrawardine the land rises gently to offer a commanding view of the countryside around Montford. At the head of the sandy lane was a cluster of houses and a sandstone church. Shrewsbury lay 4 miles to the east, but my resting place for that night would be the campsite at Montford Bridge, only a mile down the lane, where the B4380 and a recent section of the A5 cross the Severn. After a long hot day in the sun, and 12 miles behind me, I blew up my airbed and lay there for some duration. It was a while before I had the strength or the willpower to take myself the 200 yards to the post office and general store.

From Montford Bridge, the River Severn does an enormous set of loops before it almost completely encircles Shrewsbury. I decided to forgo this bit of riparian wandering and bused my way into the town. I wanted time to see not only some of Shrewsbury, but also the remains of the Roman town of Viroconium out on the east side of the city. This may be an odd revelation, but I hadn't been on a bus for years, so I was glad that there were two other people waiting at the stop. We waited for only ten minutes next to a shelter that resembled a garden shed

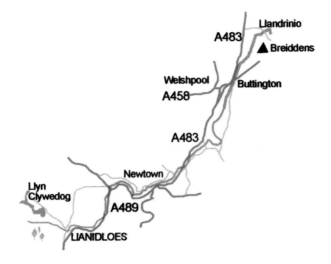

Map of the River Severn, showing its start in the hills above Llanidloes. Between Newtown and Buttington, the 'Way' follows the route of the Montgomery canal, as the Severn and 'Monty run parallel and often exceedingly close.

Shrewsbury Castle.

before a single-decker country bus came zipping around the corner. I bustled on with the locals, my rucksack and a handful of change.

We rattled off along extremely narrow country lanes, hurtling around bends and scraping against bushes and trees. Through the window I watched as cabbage- and corn-fields passed in a blur, and I looked to see if the other passengers were equally impressed with this rate of travel. Some forced smiles showed more than a hint of fear, while one regular traveller joked that our driver used to do Formula One racing before coming to the buses. Most of us gripped the chrome handrails as we bumped and swayed, wearing out a set of brakepads on stops and bends. Nevertheless the short, swift ride came to an abrupt end as we came to the outskirts of Shrewsbury and then the terminus, where crowds swarmed about the various stops and information centre. Arriving at an unknown city always provokes feelings of bewilderment tinged with excitement. I then discovered that the next bus out to the old Roman town of Viroconium was not for another two hours; plenty of time to get an unhealthy fried breakfast and then wander around the old sandstone castle and library, which is almost opposite.

I stood opposite the fine stone-built library with its mullioned windows, that was formerly a rather grand Grammar School where Charles Darwin, amongst others, was educated.

The castle, not many yards from the library, couldn't have been better sited. The River Severn provided protection for the town on three sides, while the castle on a prominent position filled the gap. The medieval castle was restored 200 years ago by Thomas Telford, and its warm red blocks are easy on the eye. The battlemented walls surround a pleasant garden of well-cut lawns and colourful flower tubs. A well-appointed bench dedicated to Violet Lucy Thomas was perfect for appreciating the scene before taking a look at a fabulous stone tower wonderfully called 'Laura's Tower', where one can get a great view of the river below. After breakfast, it was time to catch the bus to Viroconium, which is close to the river and the village of Wroxeter, about 6 miles east out of Shrewsbury.

When you get off the bus at the crossroads, you are right next to the ruins, while opposite is a useful information centre and museum run by English Heritage. The surrounding landscape, though firmly fixed in the present, still has an aura of timelessness about it, a bit like St. Peter's church. Away to the east is the solitary mound of the Wrekin at 407 metres, while south are the hills of Caer Caradoc and the Long Mynd. The Wrekin saw the last stand of the ancient tribes of the Cornovii, as the Roman army subdued the Midlands. Then, about the year AD 58, the Roman General Seutonius Paulinus established a large fortress for the 14th Legion near the ford here on the Severn. Some years after that, the 20th Legion took residence until AD 90, or CE if you prefer, when the legion demolished the

The Roman ruins of Viroconium, near the Severn-side village of Wroxeter. A hint of the Wrekin can be seen in the background.

fortress and moved further north to Chester. The place then grew as a Roman town for the next 300 years until it was finally abandoned some time before the Norman Conquest. Visitors are now able to see the layout of the town, and the visible remains of the Basilica, baths, forum and market, which all contribute to providing a glimpse into the splendour and importance of this remarkable piece of Roman Britain. I spent a couple of hours around the ruins and then caught the bus to Buildwas and another ruin – its Abbey.

The driver dropped me off on the north side of Buildwas Bridge. The turbulent rushes of a narrow waterway are now long gone and the river is a wide and mature watercourse. Today there is a substantial bridge at this point, built in 1905 to replace the one built by Telford, which in its turn replaced the much older bridge built by the monks and destroyed by the floods of 1795. Destructive floods have always been part of the Severn story, but perhaps not as frequent as they are in modern times. The afternoon was speeding by, so after a quick tour and photograph of the Abbey, I walked the last 2 miles into Ironbridge. As I approached this well-known historic place, and its even more famous bridge, the sun came out to reveal the magnificent blooms and lawns of Dale End Park; and I found a place to stay not far out of town.

The Cistercian Abbey at Buildwas; founded in 1135 and connected to the abbey in Furness, Cumbria.

IRONBRIDGE

Ironbridge is one of those places where you need several days to explore, for there is so much to see and do, and that's before you step foot into one of the several museums and craft places. It's not too hard to imagine why this quiet wooded valley was the birthplace of the Industrial Revolution, for the clues are still there, though somewhat hidden. For, only 200 years ago, this emerald gorge was filled with smoke by day and the glow of sparking furnaces by night. One might conclude that the early industrial entrepreneurs were in some kind of race to tear open the earth, uncover its hidden treasures and go on to make as much money as possible.

For some years now there has been an excellent pay and display car park on the southern side of the iron bridge (from whence came the town's excellent name), and from where a good view of the bridge can be had. The walk into Coalport some 2 miles downstream can be taken either side of the River Severn, but the southern side generally follows the course of the old Severn Valley rail track, now called the Silkin Way, and is the quieter option (though, if you wish to view certain places of interest such as the Inclined Plane or the Tar Tunnel, you will need to swap sides.) This can be done either at the iron bridge, the

Jackfield new bridge, the footbridge near the Inclined Plane, or at Coalport. At this point I shall only mention the basics of the iron bridge, for its history, design and construction is recounted in what was the old toll office, on the southern side of the bridge. The bridge was built to unite the busy industrial operations that had developed on both sides of the river that included Broseley and Benthall on the southern side, and Coalbrookdale and Madeley on the north. But, because a bridge of iron had never been made before, there was great debate about what materials and design should be used. Some wanted a traditional bridge, made of brick or stone. Finally a design by Thomas Pritchard of Shrewsbury won the day, with strong backing from John 'Iron Mad' Wilkinson, and Abraham Darby the Third, who went on to do the casting in 1779.

Certainly it is iron that the gorge is now world-famous for, because the whole valley has long been designated a World Heritage Site, and the tourist blurb proclaims that its bridge is on a par with other famous sites such as the pyramids of Egypt – and rightly so. Iron production was under way in this valley by 1322, when Walter de Caldebrook paid Wenlock Priory 6s to dig for sea coal in the brook holes (le brocholes) and later in 1544, there is mention of a Smith Place and Caldebrook Smithy, where iron was being made in 'blooms'. From Elizabethan times onward, iron works in the gorge simply grew in number and output. Up to the 1700s all iron was made using charcoal, which meant that vast swathes of forest were being cut down.

Many had tried to use coal to smelt iron but unfortunately it didn't reach the high temperatures required that charcoal did. That is until Abraham Darby the First came to Ironbridge. He solved that thorny problem by first turning the coal into coke, and thus the trees were saved – well at least from charcoal production.

Approaching Ironbridge. The breadth of the Severn shows to advantage as it flows through the gorge and past the bridge.

Looking along Ironbridge's shops from the north side of the bridge.

So, coal replaced charcoal, and iron manufacture stepped up a gear, and now on our way to Coalport we can view the Bedlam Furnaces and Tile Manufactory amongst other attractions.

After crossing the bridge to admire its lofty views across the Severn, I made my way east through the town, past the Bedlam Furnaces to the new Jackfield Bridge. This cantilever and cable design from the late twentieth century is in marked contrast to its more venerable neighbour. Its architectural merits are debatable, but it certainly does the job. I was now on my way to Coalport China Museum, for in this locality, some of the world's most famous and lovely porcelain was produced, and the remains of the old works now form the museum. First though is the Inclined Plane; and to the right of that the Tar Tunnel, a source of natural bitumen. To your right you will spot perhaps the most unique length of canal in the country, not only from its juxtaposition to the river, but also for its brevity.

THE HAY INCLINED PLANE

Essentially an inclined plane is a railway going up a hill. Here the railway overcomes the hilly terrain and links canals at top and bottom. At the top, a lock was cleverly constructed so that as the water emptied out, a short boat was lowered onto a set of carriage wheels, which could be then lowered or raised on the track. This particular plane is 1,050ft long, and copes with a height difference of 207ft. In the past, wooden rails were used for short horse-drawn rail routes, but iron was substituted for wood in this area from 1768 onward. Richard Trevithick records them in use by the Dale Company in a letter to Mr Davies Gilbert on 22 August 1802. The very short Coalport Canal served as a link from the bottom of the plane, parallel with the river to the Coalport factory.

At this point I will make a small reference to a gentleman referred to earlier, one John Wilkinson, for he was one of the great iron masters of this era. Wilkinson had several iron works; one was in Bilston in the Black Country, and a second just over the river in Broseley. His company made many items, amongst which were cannons. However, not content with selling them to his own government, it is said that he sneaked some off down the river to the French, which was a bit naughty when you consider the political climate of the time. It is not clear whether he went to France by invitation or to escape, but he did go, and there he set up another iron works to teach the French how to bore cannons. Anyhow, years later, Wilkinson came back to the Gorge and made probably the first iron barge, launching it ceremonially into the river. Sitting in his home in Broseley on 17 July 1798, Wilkinson wrote, 'Yesterday week my iron boat was launched. It answers all my expectations and has convinced the unbelievers who were nine hundred and ninety nine in a thousand. It will be a nine day wonder, and then be like Columbus's egg.'

RIVER TRAFFIC

Historically the River Severn carried a lot of freight, which is now conspicuous by its total absence. During those busy early years, Shrewsbury, Coalbrookdale (Coalbrookdale was known as such prior to the building of the iron bridge) Broseley, Bewdley, Stourport (after 1772), and Gloucester, were the great centres through which trade flowed. This trade included lead, iron in its various forms, bricks and pottery, tiles, hay, hops, cider, timber and basic foodstuffs. The *Gentleman's* magazine of 1758 said : 'This River, being justly esteemed the second in Britain, is of great importance on account of its trade; being navigated by vessels of large burden more than 160 miles from the sea. Upwards of 100,000 tons of coal alone were annually shipped from the collieries around Broseley and Madeley.'

In 1756, two years earlier, an account was taken of all the vessels and their owners operating on the River Severn, but for brevity I shall only mention the local ones of specific interest. They are Broseley with fifty-five owners with eighty-seven vessels, Benthall with eight owners and thirteen vessels, and

The Hay Inclined Plane and start of the Coalport Canal.

The Coalport Museum and its canal, running parallel with the River Severn.

Coalport Bridge; two miles downstream from Ironbridge.

Madeley Wood with twenty-one owners and operating thirty-nine vessels. Oddly enough there were none for either Coalport or Ironbridge, which reveals where the population resided at that time. Water depth along the upper reaches of the Severn was a perennial problem, and Thomas Telford was called in towards the end of the eighteenth century to try and make the river more navigable by a system of weirs and dredging. But the locals resented paying tolls for all seasons of the year, so nothing happened. Many of the owners and crews of the day were notorious for their goings-on, being described in one book as 'primitive in their habits, content to waste idly for extended periods', and 'that they were hard drinkers and heavy swearers'. It is also apparent that they were devious in their duties, for there were continual complaints that weights were under, and tickets falsified. During this time many of the boats were pulled along the river by rough men known as 'bow haulers'. Richard Reynolds was so appalled by this slavish occupation that he obtained an Act of Parliament for the proper construction of towing paths in order that horses could be used instead.

Across the river from the Inclined Plane via a footbridge is Maws Craft Centre, an ideal spot to spend an hour or two, and there is a café for light snacks. In the past this was Maws Tile Works (1852–1970). The Maws Tile factory was opened by George and Arthur Maw when they moved to Broseley to take advantage of the better clay and cheaper coal than was to be found at their other factory in Worcester. By the 1880s, the company was at its peak and making the most popular encaustic floor tiles for an astonishing clientele that included the

High Town, Bridgnorth.

Royal Family, Alexander II of Russia, two maharajahs, nine dukes, twelve earls, several railway companies, plus many other public and private buildings. The company was the largest in the world at the end of the nineteenth century, but with the recession following the First World War, and then the loss of the local railway, the firm declined and finally closed its doors in 1970.

Pottery is sadly no longer made in the Severn Valley, but in the past the region was famous for its clay, both red and white. Broseley was once a centre for the production of clay pipes (smoking that is) especially from the 1600s onward; in fact, in King James's time, the expression 'will you take a Broseley' was a well-known phrase for smoking a pipe. In 1862, a Mr Thursfield wrote, 'I have in my possession about 400 different shaped pipe bowls, which have mostly been picked up in the immediate vicinity of Broseley.'

I walked off towards Bridgnorth, another wonderful old town on the banks of the River Severn. Almost as soon as I started walking, the heavens opened and after a mile or two I was drenched through, so I thumbed a lift from a passing farmer, who thankfully allowed me to travel in the back of his pickup. It wasn't the most comfortable drive, but after a quarter of an hour I was dropped off in High Town, Bridgnorth.

Bridgnorth is comprised of two towns essentially; the one on the high ground that overlooks the river, and the one below. They are conveniently known as High Town and Low Town. Due to the size of the place, and the fact that it is a well-recognised tourist location, I looked around for a place to stay. and that is where I quickly came undone, for that weekend there was a religious celebration

A cliff railway connects High and Low Town, and is a fine way to travel between the two. This view looks past the railway to the river as it flows south from Ironbridge.

The remains of the castle at High Town. The castle was besieged by Cromwell's army during the civil war and blown up when the Royalists surrendered.

being held, and there wasn't a bed to be had for miles. There was only one thing to do – I rang my wife who kindly came and picked me up and took a very wet guy home. It wasn't the end that I had envisioned, but that's how life is on occasion. And as we drove home I wondered if the opportunity would come again where I could walk some more of the fabulous River Severn.

10

Fradley and Fazeley

Today, both Fradley and Fazeley are busy Midland Canal junctions. Fazeley is home to the modern regional headquarters of British Waterways – sorry, the Canals and Rivers Trust; one has to keep up with the changes – while its northern neighbour Fradley, some 10 miles away, carefully clings to its historic buildings which exude an unmistakeable old world charm. Still, time changes everything, and Fradley now features a nature centre and walk, craft shops and at least two cafés to keep the tourists rolling in and satisfied. Nevertheless, a handful of old photographs and a look at their individual histories take us into a very different world.

When the first canal companies started to plot and construct the early canals in the Midlands at the end of the eighteenth century, it seemed inevitable that a link would be made somewhere on the Trent and Mersey (T&M) Canal near Fradley. For Fradley was a seemingly unimportant rural location on that early waterway, but it was the southernmost point on the T&M and ideal, therefore, for anyone wishing to take a canal south. These were the days when rival canal companies were at each other's throats, where each zealously promoted plans and raised money to construct the projects that were close to their individual entrepreneurial hearts. Some ideas naturally fell by the wayside, such as the plan to take a canal from Fazeley into the Walsall coalfields. Nevertheless, the T&M Company definitely desired a link with the southern half of the country, while the Coventry and Oxford wanted to link up with the T&M. The growing Birmingham Canal Company, always on the lookout to expand its business and influence, was also keen on having better links with the growing national network, but they were always going to oppose any canal company that threatened their dominance and their profits. In the end, the fledgling Birmingham and Fazeley Company decided that it was advantageous to join its larger and more powerful rival, and a start was made on the link from Birmingham to Fradley via Fazeley.

A well-preserved crane at Fradley hints at its commercial past.

British Waterways' maintenance yard during the 1950s, when all manner of canal furniture including lock gates were manufactured here. This is an interesting view of an early canal cruiser with a working boat behind.

A view across the junction at the start of the Coventry canal, with dilapidated building and 1950s car.

Junction lock and footbridge around 1950.

Things didn't go smoothly on the Coventry or the Fazeley canals however. After the Act for the Coventry Canal was passed in January 1768, Brindley was appointed to supervise construction, but due to his vast workload, he was hardly ever there. Worked dragged on with many difficulties and failures, and in the end the Coventry Company gave him the sack – the only canal company ever to do so, though others were sorely tempted. The contractor who took on the work of building the later Fazeley Canal was John Pinkerton, who, incidentally, was also to do some poor work on the Dudley Tunnel. Not many months went by before his workmanship was being seriously examined by the Birmingham Company.

An enormous battle over money and shoddy workmanship then erupted, and in the end the Birmingham Company removed Pinkerton from the job and finished the canal themselves. The link from Birmingham to Fradley was finally made in 1789, and a year later to Oxford and the Thames.

As soon as the link to London and the North was possible, both junctions quickly became important, and two of the long-distance carriers, Pickford's

The Swan in all its glory. The imprisoned boatmen in the Christina Collins murder case were probably held in the Swan or the building next door.

Fazeley Junction around 1950, with the junction house opposite.

and Bache's, who transported every kind of merchandise, and even occasionally passengers, speedily opened depots at these points. The carriers ran a fixed timetable for the convenience of their customers, and boats stopped at a whole host of stations along the route. Both the Trent and Mersey and Coventry Canal Companies built cottages for their workers, which included wharfingers and company agents who kept an eager eye on the goods, timing of boats and the paperwork. Warehouses were built for the storing of goods, while the wharves were constantly busy with the loading, unloading and the transhipment of goods. At Fradley, it was inevitable that the junction needed a public house and The Swan was one of the first buildings on the site.

In the late eighteenth and nineteenth centuries, fly boats carrying perishable and high-value merchandise travelled day and night past these junctions with usually a four-man crew that worked a shift pattern. In 1839, one of Pickford's crews were held temporarily in handcuffs at Fradley overnight for the murder of Christina Collins, who had been travelling with the boat as a passenger from Liverpool to London. In the second half of the twentieth century British Waterways had a lively workshop depot at Fradley that dealt with all the local maintenance issues, such as the manufacture of lock gates, boat repair and water

Peel's wharf and the Canal and River Trust (previously British Waterways) headquarters for the region.

management. Nevertheless, towards the end of the century, waterway policy changed, and those buildings had a complete makeover. The buildings have now been converted into craft shops, plus a café that caters for the thousands of visitors that come to the site. A large iron crane sitting at the water's edge still hints at the work that went on at this attractive location.

Of course today, Fradley junction is still busy with short and long-term moorings, while a dry dock is used for boat maintenance. Many other visitors arrive by car to walk around the nature trail, shop at the craft centre, watch the waterway activity or visit The Swan, which does a roaring trade – especially in summer months – with ales and meals. Various internet sites give the pub a thumbs-up, and the most recent managers seem to have built a reputation for friendliness. Their latest menu offers a wide range of dishes with vegetarian options and a menu for children. I went along on a beautiful sunny day during the winter to get some fabulous snow and ice photos. Fazeley doesn't have the charm of its more rural rival, but the old mill factory and the junction house certainly point a finger at its industrial heritage. J.M. Pearson in *Canal Companions* points out that Sir Robert Peel (father of the Prime Minister) opened a mill at this junction for the spinning of cotton and printing of calico. That early mill has, however, long been overshadowed by the five-storey mill built in 1883, which now stands as silent testament to a past industrial world. So in essence, our present junctions have seen a complete alteration of purpose since the days of their commercial activity, but still manage to provide a welcome diversion from twenty-first-century life.

11

Jim Edwards: Boating Memories of the 1930s

This is the story of boats, places, and the people associated with them. In 2012 a historic working boat came up for sale at a brokerage for almost £45,000. It was named *Spade*; no not after the digging implement, but the card suit. It is unlikely that anyone viewing the craft, either physically or on the internet, would have an inkling into its past, unless possibly the traditional boat cabin with pull-down bed and stove gave it away.

Noah and Mary Edwards at Bunberry locks on the Shropshire Union Canal with their family and boats *Spade* and *Welcome*. They worked for The Midlands and Coast Canal Carrying Company in the mid-1930s. Noah is on the left holding the rope, while Mary is in the background. Notice the two horses at the lock side.

The *Spade* – named after the card symbol, not the digging implement, with Noah on the cabin top and wife, Mary, at the tiller; Wolverhampton – sometime during the 1930s.

Maesbury Marsh, on the Montgomery Canal near Oswestry; looking from the canal bridge towards the wharf and warehouses. Mr and Mrs Edwards worked from here for A.A. Peat and Company during the First World War.

Jim has always been proud of his three older brothers, two of them looking very smart here as children, who went on to lead active service lives during the Second World War. Tom was in the Royal Navy, Alf was involved in the D-Day landings, while another brother, Bill, worked on the emergency dock called Mullberry.

Barbridge Junction in the days when there was a warehouse right over the canal. Jim recalls boats tying up here and unloading.

Today, this 62ft boat has a well-fitted kitchen, a largish living area, bathroom with hip bath, shower and toilet; and yet eight years ago the same space would have probably been filled with sacks of flour, or another commodity, and its tiny cabin crammed with a hungry working family preparing their daily meals.

Close to Top Lock in Wolverhampton is a warehouse, ancillary buildings and a small basin now utilised for travelling leisure boats. The warehouse is currently a nightclub, but in former years it was first the headquarters of the Midland and

Hack Green. It was here that they had trouble getting their boat alongside the towing path and Alf had to use one of their poles to vault onto the bank.

Coast Canal Carrying Company. The connection between boat and location is the Edward family. Jim Edwards is now in his eighties, but he remembers with fondness working as a young boy, along with his parents and siblings during the mid-war decade of the 1930s. The family's canal story, however, starts a little before that, at the start of the twentieth century.

In 1908, Jim's mother Mary and their family were thrown out of their Wolverhampton home by bailiffs for rent arrears, for there was no government assistance in those days if you were unfortunate enough to be out of work. Mary's two older brothers managed to get work on a narrowboat, and this is how she met her husband-to-be, Noah Edwards, just before the First World War. While the war in the trenches went on, they worked for a small family-based carrying company called A.A. Peate, based in the idyllic border village of Maesbury Marsh, near Oswestry on the Montgomery Canal. A.A. Peate had a handful of boats, and were fully occupied carrying unmilled wheat and flour from the mills at Ellesmere Port to the mill in Maesbury Marsh, and delivering foodstuffs to the farms dotted along the Llangollen and Shropshire Union Canals. *Margaret* was the last boat that Peates ever had, and it was captained by Jim's uncle, Tom Wilday.

As you may be aware, boaters rarely stayed with one company for long, and by the 1930s the growing family had gone to work for the Midlands and Coast (M&C) Canal Carrying Company based on the main line off Broad Street in Wolverhampton. Jim and Joe Edwards were only slips of lads, but they spent their long days driving the horse, and handling the tiller or any other boating chores.

Wolverhampton Top Lock, with its basins and wharves, was a very busy spot in those days, with queues of boats waiting to descend the 21. Due to the size of the family – Noah and Mary had twelve children in all – the company had them on two horse-drawn boats, the *Spade* and the *Welcome*. Spade was built just a few years earlier in 1929 by Crichton and Co. at Salteney on the River Dee near Chester. It was one of four iron-sided, elm-bottom boats ordered by M&C, who started operating in Wolverhampton in 1922.

Midlands and Coast operated some seventy boats over the years, carrying a wide range of cargoes to many destinations, until they were taken over by Fellows, Morton and Clayton in 1939. As for the Edwards family, well, conditions were rather cramped for sleeping, but fortunately several of the smaller children could be accommodated in the tiny fore cabins. Trade was brisk, with many runs up and down the 'Shroppie' from Ellesmere Port, carrying wheat, flour and foodstuffs into Wolverhampton and Birmingham. Sometimes they took on chocolate crumb at Knighton and delivered it to the big Cadbury's depot at Bourneville on the Worcester and Birmingham Canal. On other days they took metal tubes from the manufactories along the Dudley number two canal up the Shroppie to Ellesmere Port, or brought soda from the River Weaver, close to the Anderton lift, back into Birmingham. Every week was different, though the locks and junctions along the Shropshire Union came to be as familiar to the youngsters as the backs of their hands, compounded by their non-attendance in school and constant attention to the world of the waterways.

Apollo was the second powered boat to be used by Midlands and Coast during the 1930s. Later it went to FMC, and then as a tug for Ernie Thomas. More lately it has been used as a tour boat at Shipley Wharf on the Leeds and Liverpool canal, for the aptly named Apollo Canal Cruises.

A gathering of the six brothers during the 1980s. At the back are Tom, Fred, Alf, Bill, Jim and Joe.

Winter brought its own set of difficulties to boat people, and one winter was especially etched into Jim's memory, an experience impossible to forget. The family had just delivered tubes to Ellesmere Port and were between Chester and Beeston when the temperature dropped rapidly. They moored pretty much in the middle of nowhere, and when dawn broke, both boats were well frozen into the bank. Not even the courageous work of the iceboats could get them out of that situation; all they could do was to make themselves as comfortable as possible and wait for two things; the company to send them some money, and the thaw. Fortunately *Spade* had its own range, a lifesaver during winter months, while not too far away was a country pub that supplied them with drinking water, and a village shop to supply food and other necessities. The kids slept head-to-tail for warmth. The thaw came eight weeks later. Summers, however, could be equally delightful, when the youngsters slept on straw sacks under the stars on top of the cargo.

From the photographs, it is clear that Noah was not a powerfully built man, but he was as strong as an ox, and would unload a 25-ton cargo almost on his own. And at five o'clock every morning he would wake everyone up with his call – LOOK ALIVE! Meanwhile Mary cooked for the whole family on the small coal-fired range in *Spade*'s cabin. At lunchtime trays of food would be left for the trailing boat somewhere near the towing path.

Jim Edwards in his eighties in 2011. Joe is the only other surviving brother who lives near Telford.

The headquarters of Midlands and Coast Canal Carriers during the 1930s was in Wolverhampton. It later came under Fellows Morton and Clayton, who took the work over, before becoming British Waterways. Today it is a nightclub.

The arm and small office belonging to Midlands and Coast Canal Carriers Company.

Wolverhampton Top Lock, the buildings have not unchanged since the Edwards' day, though the surrounding area has altered considerably.

The coal-fired range fitted to many narrowboats was tiny by modern standards, but an essential piece of kit. It saved the lives of many boatmen such as the Edwards brothers during frozen months of the year by providing warmth and hot food and drinks.

During the 1930s, most working-class families saw hardship of one kind or another; the youngest Edwards brothers remember vividly wearing torn trousers and only one pair of shoes between the two of them. Jim and Joe were always fond of football, and on at least one occasion Jim wore the left while his brother wore the right. But technology was moving on, and this was the decade when many carrying companies started to experiment with boats powered by the new diesel engines. In 1936, the Edwards were given the *Apollo* to tow *Spade*. *Apollo* was built by John Crichton in 1929, and fitted with a Petter 18HP engine. Unfortunately the early Petters were prone to breaking down, causing some captains to rue the day that they lost their four-legged friends.

Two years later, Noah and Mary decided that after more than three decades of working the inland waterways they had had enough, and went for a life on dry land. Jim went off to night school where he learned to read and write, and had a distinguished career on the railways. After forty-nine years and nine months, in 1990, he was awarded the British Empire Medal. In later years, several members of the family have taken holidays on the narrow canals, and it has been a pleasure to see two of the boats that the family used for freight, surviving into the age of the leisure trade.

12

Boulton and Watt go on a Canal Trip, August 1799

The famous duo of Matthew Boulton and James Watt are well known for the introduction of the steam engine, but they were equally passionate about, and instrumental in, promoting the first Midland Canals. When Boulton entertained visitors to his amazing factory in Soho, Birmingham – which often included foreign aristocratic dignitaries – he occasionally arranged fabulous canal trips to impress his customers. One such trip, complete with orchestra, took place in 1799. In the August of that year, Soho House prepared itself to receive the Russian Ambassador, Count Woronoff, and his entourage. The guests were shown around the factory, taken to the theatre to see *Hamlet*, and then the next day taken by carriage to the wharf. Boulton wrote enthusiastically some days later:

I had previously planned and arranged a secret expedition, having provided two Compleat seating Barges with Covered Cabins and sash windows in each. One of them I sent a little forward, out of sight with a trumpet, 2 French Horns, 2 Clarinets, 2 German flutes, 2 Bassoons, 2 hautboys [oboes] and a large double drum.

As soon as the Count was seated in the cabin, he said – 'Hark, I hear music.' The windows were opened and the swell increased as we drew near. He at length exclaimed –'This is delightful, and I am confidant this is my dear friend's plans.'

We passed the Band and sailed into the foundry [Smethwick] walked round and re-embarked with the band playing before us. In about an hour we arrived at the Brades [Oldbury] and saw one of our engines forging steel, a tilting forge, grinding plates of steel and sad irons, grinding gun barrels; boring them and also grinding spectacle glasses. After the interesting sight was over, we adjourned to Mr Hunt's house where we found a large table in the parlour served with joints of cold roast Lamb, Tongues, Pigeon pies, with a variety of Pastry and fruit, which was

Statue of Boulton, Watt and Murdock in Birmingham.

Site of the Soho Foundry, Birmingham Main Line Canal, Smethwick.

Soho House, Birmingham, the home of Matthew Boulton. Now a visitor centre and museum. (Courtesy Soho House Museum)

Matthew Boulton.

also unexpected. The band played in the hall while we dined, and after dinner we had some loyal songs.

We again entered our boats, and by the assistance of the Musick, we increased the apparent population of the country immensely. After stopping several times to see Coal Mines, iron furnaces, Fire Engines [Steam Engines] and sundry works, we at length entered the regions of darkness which I dispelled by many torches which I had provided. New and immense caverns opened as we proceeded, through

Part of the old Soho Foundry.

The dining room at Soho. This is where Boulton entertained his famous guests such as Erasmus Darwin and Joseph Priestly. (Courtesy Soho House Museum)

James Watt.

Old Line at Dudley Port, Boulton's marvellous trip passed this way en route to the Dudley Tunnel and Limestone Caverns.

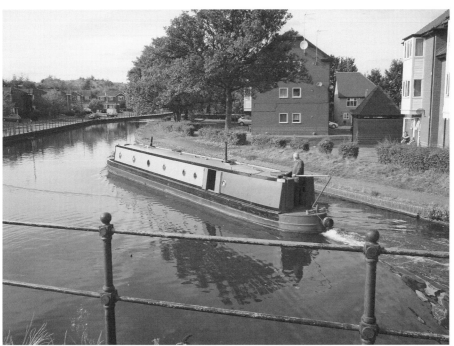

which we often espied through openings, the inhabitants of ye earth looking down upon us. The Band of Musick played al the time & beautifully echoed from the Salons of Erebus (Greek God of Underworld and darkness).

Perhaps Boulton was inspired by Handel's Water Music – who knows, but the day out, from Winson Green wharf, to the cavernous limestone workings in Tipton (near the present Black Country Museum), were designed to impress, and impress they did.

This trip took place on the old Brindley Line, as the Telford New Main Line was still thirty years in the future. Nevertheless the original summit three locks had been removed, so they would only have had to negotiate the three Smethwick locks that are still in existence.

13

Horseboating: Yesterday and Today

In the early days of the canal age all boats and barges were towed by horse, mule or occasionally a pair of donkeys, and a lot of the surviving buildings and features of canals were designed with horsepower in mind. Working a boat with a horse required considerable skill and knowledge, and lots of practice. A horse towing a boat with a rope from the bank was actually a very efficient means of transport because at a steady walk a horse could pull fifty times as much cargo in a boat as it could in a cart or wagon on rough roads. This huge improvement in transport efficiency led to the great canal building era in the eighteenth century, which in turn paved the way for the Industrial Revolution and modern industry. Horses were the prime movers of this great change and they remained at work right through to the middle of the twentieth century.

A restored Gifford at the Oldbury gathering during 2006, fifty years after the Thomas Clayton fleet stopped carrying.

Caggy Stevens of Tipton; probably the last man to horseboat into the second half of the twentieth century. The repair yard at Tipton is still called Caggy's yard, today though Caggy left the earthly waterways scene some years since.

Many horses were lost from accidents during the late nineteenth and early twentieth centuries. Here officials are trying to rescue a fallen horse from a pound in the Ryders Green flight of locks during the 1960s. (D. Wilson)

A collar-fitting demonstration to a boat horse at the Black Country Living Museum.

So, how many horses do you think worked on the inland waterways of Britain in the past? And how many horses are pulling boats today? Accurate statistics are hard to come by, but I do know that there were roughly between three and four million horses ready for work in Victorian Britain, there being 300,000 in London alone. One very sad but amazing statistic states that 800,000 horses were killed during the First World War, a deplorable number. Now in the twenty-first century we are down to a national population of about 600,000 animals. Still, if I were a guessing man, I would say there must have been some 15,000 horses, mules or donkeys hauling boats of one kind or another during the heyday of the canals in the nineteenth century. Steam propulsion was tried during the middle of the nineteenth century with limited success, and diesel engines burgeoned in number from the first quarter of the twentieth century onward.

HORSES, MULES OR DONKEYS?

In Britain the horse tended to reign supreme, however, during the eighteenth century the Duke of Bridgwater, amongst others, attempted to breed mules; in fact the first boat to travel the Duke's canal in 1761 was drawn by two mules working side by side. But as time went by horses tended to be preferred because they cope with cold weather much better, and are generally more reliable.

Boat carriers in general were never particularly interested in the breed of horse as long as it did the job, and had the temperament that allowed basic training. A horse with natural intelligence, though, was always going to be an asset, especially after getting into a routine; and the horse that could go 'Bacca', a term that meant that the horse would carry on without supervision, while the steerer leaned back and had a smoke, was always prized. One of the essential features of training was to get the horse used to getting a full load under way; this was called hauling off, and required the animal to lean forward into his collar to make a smooth transition to regular walking speed. This was not always easy in confined spaces around bridges and locks, and some horses never quite got the hang of it. A horse with a vicious or unpredictable nature was always going to be trouble, and a handful of boatmen and women were actually killed or injured by such creatures. Ill-treatment was, however, usually the other way round, as the animal regularly worked a ten- to twelve-hour day, and in some cases beyond its

The lovely Llangollen wharf with its café and gift shop; now managed by the Furniss family.

Here the Llangollen horseboat is preparing to take passengers on a ride towards the Horseshoe Falls.

Trevor is four miles downstream from Llangollen, and the motorboat takes regular trips to this special location along with its big draw, the Pontcysyllte Aqueduct that straddles the valley of the River Dee.

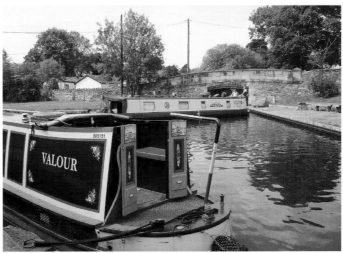

natural strength. Of course, much depended on the policy of the canal company or indeed the family that operated the boat. Sensible carriers made sure that their horses were seen regularly by the blacksmith or farrier for new shoes, that they were watered regularly, and fed a mixture of hay, oats and grain, though the diet was often improved with portions of vegetables.

Many horses though were worked by people who were too poor or unfeeling to care for them, and they were whipped from the start of a journey to its finish, whereas more kindly families treated their animals as a respected, even loved member of their group. Many owners were proud to show them off in local and national shows, with much attention to grooming and polished tack, and though

Pleasure boat crossing the Pontcysyllte Aqueduct.

Jenny Roberts of the Godalming Packet Boat Company with Buddy and boat *Iona*.

horse deaths were common, smaller companies, and especially those that just ran the one boat and its horse, realised that the untimely death of their horse could put them out of business. Fortunately, the treatment of horses started to improve after the first Act to prevent cruelty to horses in 1823, and later after the establishment of the RSPCA.

Where once there were thousands of horses working the waterway network, today there are only about two dozen available and trained to do the job.

On the River Wey with *Iona*, this time being pulled by Ben.

They are divided up between five family companies that operate pleasure trip boats, and the Horseboating Society. The Black Country Museum also has one or two.

So if you fancy doing something completely different with your family this year, a ride on a genuine horseboat through delightful countryside may just fit the bill. The five companies I mentioned earlier are spread around the country, and I shall start with the one that operates out of Llangollen wharf amidst the mountains of North Wales, simply because I have been there several times and the scenery is spectacular.

Llangollen wharf sits at the canal side on the east side of the bustling Welsh town. The canal with its historic wharf boasts a splendid and commanding view over the town, the River Dee and the historic railway station. The canal itself has travelled 4 magnificent miles from Trevor and the famous Pontcysyllte Aqueduct. The crystal clear water flows through Llangollen from its start point 2 miles further along at the Horseshoe Falls. The falls was a clever device of Thomas Telford, who ingeniously tapped into the River Dee at this leafy location in order to supply the canal with most of its water.

Horse-drawn boats have been operating out of Llangollen wharf since 1884, which is probably a distinction for the horseboat story. The company

The Brind family, who manage the horse boating operation from the basin in Tiverton, Devon.

(Welsh Canal Holiday Craft) is presently owned by Bill and Ros Knapp, and along with Bill's brother Peter and family they operate two horseboats and a new motorboat that takes regular trips to the Pontcysyllte Aqueduct, plus they have a day-hire boat. The two horse-drawn craft take regular trips to the Horseshoe Falls, and the company keep six horses on rotational duties for this work. As you can imagine, having six horses is a full-time job in itself. They have to be walked to and from the wharf each day from the field, fed, brushed and combed, and generally cossetted, and harness work and tack have to be cleaned at the end of each working day, as do the stalls.

Llangollen wharf is one of the major attractions of this splendid market town, and the company has a delightfully situated café, serving breakfasts and light lunches throughout the day. Welsh cream teas are always available with homemade scones, and Bara Brith (sorry I haven't tried it) with jam and clotted cream. The gift shop attached to the café also stocks a variety of waterway books.

Many miles away in the heart of gorgeous Devon sits the Tiverton Canal Company, and amongst many business endeavours they operate a horse-drawn barge. The company, originally called the Grand Western Horse Boat Company, was established in 1974 by one Tony Stockwell. But since 1985 it has been successfully run by the Brind family concern; and Philip Brind, along with his wife Jacquie and family, have worked hard to expand the business.

The Tiverton Canal Park, run by Devon County Council.

The barge, *Tivertonian* at a lift bridge.

Day boats and booking office at Tiverton, Devon.

The Kennet Horse Boating Company's horse Freddie, munching cow parsley – I hope it's good for him.

Freddie working through bridge holes and hauling *Kennet Valley*.

Bywater Cruises are the second Welsh horseboat company, and operates on the gorgeous Montgomery Canal.

Their beautifully painted all-weather barge the *Tivertonian* glides peacefully along the old Grand Western Canal through the captivating environment of what is now a country park and nature reserve. Their most popular excursion is a two-and-a-half hour return, where the *Tivertonian*, with its fully licensed bar, travels through rural delights to the tiny village of East Manley. At this point the barge moors for a short spell to allow trippers to stretch their legs and maybe take a short walk to view the Brunel-designed aqueduct. Back at the capacious Tiverton town wharf, you can hire a rowing boat, Canadian canoe, self-drive boat, or simply get a bite to eat from the quirkily named Ducks Ditty café bar.

The Grand Western Canal opened in 1814 at a cost of over £220,000. It was meant to be part of a more grandiose scheme that should have linked Bristol to Exeter, but that ambitious scheme never came to fruition, and instead the canal was utilised for the local transportation of coal and limestone. Today its remaining 11 miles are perfect for walking, cycling and canoeing (there is no connection to the rest of the waterway network). The waterway was taken over by Devon County Council in 1971 as a country park, and they have done a fine job of managing the waterway and its rich environment. The water quality is excellent, due to the fresh springs that supply it, all of which contributes to a healthy home for its wildlife.

It is still possible to see traces of horseboating activity, though you have to look hard. Here at the bottom of the Spon Lane locks in West Bromwich we see a horse tethering point, and the remains of a small brick hovel that the boatmen used in bad weather.

In the past, horseboaters were very proud of their animals. Here we see a typical boatman, his horse and his boss in Tipton; early twentieth century.

The *Saturn* is the only working example of a horse-drawn Shropshire Union Fly Boat in the world. The boat has been restored and is now run by the Shropshire Union Fly Boat project. She is seen here on the Llangollen Canal in 2011.

Down in Surrey, Jenny Roberts runs the Godalming Packet Boat Company. She has been operating horse-drawn trips on the National Trust-owned River Wey since 1984, when the 72ft narrowboat *Iona* arrived on the back of a lorry. Every summer from Easter to the end of September, *Iona* carries happy members of the general public, retired groups, wedding parties and corporate groups from all over the country. The company operates one historic boat and two fine horses. Ben is a fifteen hand roan gelding who was born in 1993. After starting work pulling a trap at Brentwood, he was then purchased in 1998 to haul *Iona*, and has made several TV appearances. Buddy is a slightly older Clydesdale gelding who transferred from the Welsh operator Bywater Cruises. *Iona* has the distinction of being an original working boat with the Grand Union Canal Carrying Company. In the old days she carried coal, steel, limejuice, timber and chocolate crumb to Cadbury's wharf – but not all at the same time. She was later transferred to British Waterways. In 1960, she was used in the film *The Bargee* starring Harry H. Corbet, Ronnie Barker and Eric Sykes. In 1984 she finally came into the hands of Jenny Roberts along with the boat horse Domino, a sixteen hand skewbald shire cross, who happily continued to pull *Iona* until he retired at 25 years of age. Domino was a regular star of the small screen, starring in the Inspector Morse episode 'The Wench is Dead'. And if you are something of a canal anorak, you will know that that episode was loosely based on the murder of Christina Collins on the Trent and Mersey Canal in 1840. If you are not familiar with this true but gruesome tale, you can find the whole account of the trial and execution of the perpetrators in my book *Canal Crimes*.

Further west is the Kennet Horse Boat Company (KHBC), run by husband and wife team Stephen and Charlotte Butler. They operate the horse-drawn barge *Kennet Valley,* plus a self-steer boat *Cygnet*. They managed three horses, but recently Bonny was retired, leaving them with Freddy and a young Welsh cob. So they have recently taken on a new horse, Monty, for training. The KHBC was started in 1970, and taken over by the Butler family in 1980, working out of Kintbury. You have to admire the courage and hard work of the folk who take on such a responsible but risky project. Yes, they all love their horses, and that is probably the main attraction. But it is a risky venture, with long hours, and the vet's bills alone can be enormous. Kintbury, by the way, is a picturesque village just off the A4 between Newbury and Hungerford. So, if you wish to experience working horses in action, see the countryside from a new angle, or simply want to experience what barge life was like in the old days, why not give these companies a go.

14

John Corbett: The Salt King

During the bitter dark months of January and February 1879, England was hit by a freeze, and almost forty boats were iced up in the vicinity of the Stoke Prior Salt Works alone. Fortunately for the stranded boatmen and their hard-pressed families, a few caring individuals came to their aid. Mr Hobrough, the engineer for the Worcester and Birmingham Canal, supplied 73 quarts of hot soup and a quantity of bread on two occasions, while John Corbett of Château Impney, and owner of one of the largest salt works in the country, did the same.

But who was this John Corbett who took soup and bread to cold and hungry boat people? How did he come to be called 'The Salt King' and one of the richest men in the country? And why did he build a gorgeous French château in the heart of Worcestershire, only a stone's throw from the Droitwich Canal?

John Corbett was born in 1817, to Joseph and Hannah Corbett. Instantly he became associated with the busy Midland canals because his father ran a canal-carrying company close to the bottom of the Delph locks in Brierley Hill. John, who was the first of several children, followed his father into the canal business at the tender age of eleven after receiving a few years of elementary education.

Over the next few years the young lad learned all there was to know about operating narrowboats, and eagerly soaked up all the information on how his father's company and its customers operated. In 1840, at the age of 23, Joseph arranged for his son to become an apprentice at the nearby Ley's Ironworks, owned by Hurst and Brown, in order to expand his horizons. Six years later, with the experience of the iron industry under his belt, he returned to join his father's business as a partner.

Meanwhile, some 20 miles away and right next to the Worcester and Birmingham Canal, a good supply of salt had been discovered. One entrepreneur named William Furnival, a Cheshire man, had already set up business, just a few miles south of this position is the town of Droitwich, a town that had been a producer of salt even before the Romans arrived. Salt was always a prized

John Corbett.

Looking down the Delph Locks. John
Corbett's father's canal business was based
somewhere near the bottom lock during the
early to middle of the nineteenth century.
(K. Hodgkins)

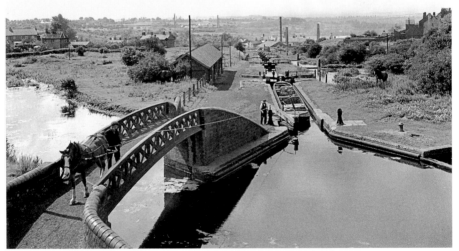

commodity to the Romans, and they built a road west, which to this day is
still called the 'salt road'. Salt production was one of the main reasons for the
construction of the Droitwich Barge Canal, but by the middle of the nineteenth
century, the salt enterprise at Stoke Prior was about to overtake it.

By 1836, when Corbett was still in Stourbridge, two rival salt companies had set
themselves up on opposite banks of the W&B Canal. They were the British Alkali

Company and the Imperial Company. The W&B Canal Company, with obvious vested interests, watched these two companies with a keen eye, and assisted their developments by constructing wharves and sluices into the works. Progress for these companies was, however, not smooth and both experienced great difficulties during the 1840s from rising competition and from contamination of the underground brine. Unfortunately for them, ground water was getting into the brine pits and rendering it almost useless.

During this period, John Corbett, as part of his father's carrying business, was involved with the British Alkali Company, both in transporting and promoting the sale of salt products. He also had a vested concern in the success of the salt trade. And from the wings, he watched with growing interest as the two rival companies struggled to deal with the twin difficulties of extraction and sale.

Stoke Wharf, now the home of Black Prince boats, but in the past a busy wharf for the handling of salt and coal.

Stoke Wharf, looking south along the W&B. The salt works of J. Corbett would have been under the bridge to the left.

Hanbury Wharf, where much salt came from the town of Droitwich and on to the W&B.

From the 1820s through to the 1840s many thousands of pounds had been invested by both companies in the salt business, and as the contamination became critical, they brought in experts to try and solve the problem. The experts didn't help, and the businesses floundered, but who would buy a company that was on the rocks?

And this was John Corbett's big gamble. He observed the demise of the two companies with an eagle eye, and when the British Alkali Company declared itself bankrupt, he purchased the whole concern for a little over £1,000. Onlookers may no doubt have thought him foolish, but Corbett had a plan, and it drew on the knowledge that he had gained from working in the iron trade. His solution to the salt contamination was simple and elegant. The brine, deep underground, was being diluted by groundwater, so he brought in engineers who sunk large cast-iron cylinders, carefully sealed and bolted together, down to the source of the natural brine deposits. The contamination was now effectively contained, and the concentrated salty fluid was then pumped to the surface and transferred to the salt pans. Here, the excess water was driven off by evaporation, leaving the prized white crystals formed some millions of years before to be dried, bagged and sold to a worldwide market.

Later, Corbett purchased the property of the Imperial Salt Company on the other side of the canal, and went on to make a fortune. Unlike many other Victorian masters, Corbett cared about his workers and he introduced a cleaner working environment, built decent homes for them (he employed about 500 people) and provided elementary education, amongst other improvements. Corbett's new management of the Worcestershire salt production, right at the side of the W&B Canal, took it to grand success. During the 1860s and 1870s, the Stoke Prior saltworks produced over 150,000 tons of fine and coarse salt each year, much of it heading initially to Gloucester and Birmingham by narrowboat. Coal came in the other direction, mainly from the close-at-hand Black Country coalfields, easily accessed via the BCN and Dudley Canal system, (it took 1 ton of coal to make 2 tons of salt), to heat the evaporating pans, and, as a consequence of this huge trade, he built up his own fleet of some fifty narrowboats.

As the business expanded (much of the salt went overseas), Corbett, for business and pleasure, became extremely fond of travelling. Leaving a competent manager behind, he crossed the Channel several times to sample the delights of Paris, and it was on one of these trips, in 1855, that he met the woman who was to become his wife. Anna Eliza O'Meara was one of two talented and beautiful daughters of the Irish diplomat William O'Meara. These young women had all the charms that French society could wish for, but the family had no money, and it didn't take their father long to recognise what a fine match it would be if one of his daughters should marry this rich and delightfully old-fashioned businessman with the Black Country accent. So Corbett was treated like a visiting royal, and soon he was entranced by the lovely Anna Eliza. Twelve months later, the couple married and settled into Stoke Grange.

One would have thought this was a fine marriage in the making; Anna was married to one of the richest men in the kingdom; she had a good-sized house

Vines Park in the centre of Droitwich – now the centre of the regeneration of the Droitwich canal system, which in the past carried many tons of salt.

The Boat and Railway, which stood opposite the salt works and is now a very popular pub that also serves the interests of the W&B Canal Society.

The fabulous Château Impney, built in 1875 for Anna Eliza Corbett. Now a hotel and conference centre.

with servants, and they had each other. Sadly, though this was not enough. Corbett wanted social status to go along with his wealth, so he dabbled in the political arena, but never really fitted in. Even with his money behind him, he took a bit of a mauling from the infinitely more sophisticated Pakingtons, who lived in the established Tory seat of Westwood Park, and they taunted the Protestant Corbett about his Catholic wife. Anna, for her part, was never satisfied with the quiet life in Worcestershire, and pined for the rich society of London and Paris.

Nevertheless, Corbett hadn't achieved his position in life by being a shrinking violet. Even though the Pakingtons boasted a legacy that went back to William the Conqueror, he had greater capital than they did, and when Anna waxed lyrical about the grand Châteaux in the Loire Valley, the Salt King had a brainwave. He would search out the best architect and build a fabulous French château right there in the heart of Worcestershire – close, but not too close to his salt works and the Worcester Canal. A mansion, in short, would elevate his own name, push Westwood Park well into second place, and please his wife all at the same time. It was a capital plan.

And so, John Corbett, the lad from Brierley Hill, purchased the Manor of Impney next to the Droitwich Canal, had the old house moved to another location and hired the French architect, August Tronquois. His brief was to construct – with no regard for expense – a grand house in the style of Louis XIII. Indeed, no expense was spared, and the ornate exterior of the building used an attractive combination of fine red and cream brick and cream Bath Stone. This wonderful exterior only hinted at the luxury to be found inside. Within those fine walls were decoratively plastered rooms, with the drawing room alone displaying reliefs of the four famous musicians – Handel, Hayden, Beethoven and Brahms. Door furniture was embellished with small cherubs, while larger golden cherubs graced the walls.

When finally installed in the house, Corbett and his wife, from their bedroom window, could gaze across a landscape that was a harmony of nature and artifice, which included the sculpted banks of the River Salwarpe. Formal gardens were punctuated with pools and fountains. The architect and owner had thought of everything, even down to the cat flaps designed into the skirting boards – Corbett was extremely fond of animals. Estimates show that as many as 3,000 people worked on the house and grounds, while a whopping £200,000 was spent in the process (in modern terms £11–12 million). And when the house was up and running, the great man employed two women whose duty it was to look after the gravel drive and rake away the horse muck so as not to detract from the splendour of it all.

Unfortunately, the initial happiness was not to last. As the years went by, Anna bore her husband five children, but the gap between them widened and they were finally separated in 1884. When a sixth child was born in 1876, John was so sure that it was not his, that he refused to acknowledge it, and rumours of it being fathered by the mother's favourite priest were too well known to be suppressed.

She took the children to a small property on the Banks of the Fowey in Cornwall, while John rattled around in his rather large French folly, selling his salt, being a shareholder of the W&B Canal and a director of the Gloucester and Berkeley Canal, and then its successor for some years, until his death in 1901.

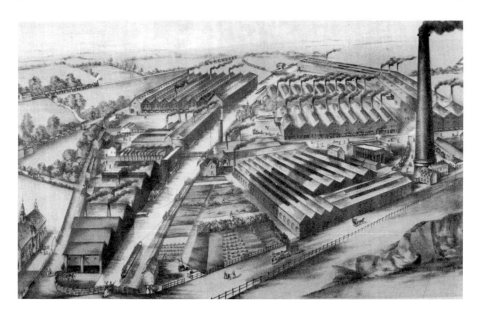

The historic Salt Works on the B&W Canal. (Rev. Alan White)

As for the salt trade, in 1894, the Salt Unions acquired half of John Corbett's fleet of narrowboats, but by the First World War that number was down to eight. Small quantities of salt were still carried by narrowboat on the Birmingham and Worcester Canal until the Second World War though salt production carried on until as late as the 1970s. Today, Chateau Impney still looks as fabulous as the day it was completed and is a fashionable hotel and events complex. It was on the market for sale in 2008 for a cool £25 million.

15

The Droitwich Story

Friday, 1 July 2011 to Sunday, 3 July, was a wonderful landmark occasion for all waterway lovers, for it saw the official opening celebrations of the perfectly restored Droitwich canals. I say canals for there are two, relatively short, but important canals that constitute one connecting link from the lower half of the Worcester and Birmingham Canal through the medieval town of Droitwich to the River Severn at Hawford. There is the 5-mile Barge Canal from Droitwich down to the Severn, and the 2-mile Droitwich Junction Canal.

Friday started with mixed sunshine and showers, a typical British day you might say, but Sunday was completely and magnificently glorious, with blue skies hovering benevolently over Droitwich, as thousands of well-wishing promenaders, and dozens of boats, made their way happily through Vines Park right in the centre of Droitwich. And just as a bonus, that weekend coincided nicely with historic Droitwich's 'Salt Day' the town's *raison d'etre*, the celebration of the town's long attachment to, and production of, that vital glittering white stuff – salt.

October 1973 and the first Inland Waterways Association volunteer work party, who 'discovered the canal to locals' amazement'. (M. Sinclair)

Looking at the Barge Lock sometime during the 1970s. The lock had basically either fallen apart or been filled with muck and rubbish intentioanlly. (M. Sinclair)

August 2008, and groundwork continues just north of the M5 motorway.

Two hundred and forty years after the Barge Canal opened on 10 March 1771, the two combined restored waterways now form a new link that makes a mini cruising circuit of 21 miles. Dubbed 'The Mid Worcestershire Ring', the loop allows boaters, cyclists, fishermen and ramblers to sample a journey through some of the best countryside the Midlands has to offer.

But before we move on too quickly with modern goings-on, let us take a look at how and why the original canals were built. The Droitwich route of just over

7 miles is indeed the amalgamation of two waterways, and a salty theme connects them and the town of Droitwich. Salt was produced in the area long before the Romans came; but it was those salt-conscious people who constructed a road across to the east to carry it away. However, narrow tracks and roads were never going to be enough to satisfy both demand and supply.

EARLY YEARS

The original Droitwich Barge Canal was surveyed by the legendary James Brindley, to transport the town's main produce of salt 5 miles down to the River Severn. It was one of only a couple of waterways that he was privileged to see finished in 1771 before his early demise the following year. Brindley was appointed Inspector of the works at £60 per year, but the man who was really responsible for the day-to-day running of the construction was John Priddey, who received £90 per annum. Work began in June 1768, pretty much the

Preparation of one of the new locks just north of the M5.

The same lock after completion in July 2011.

Dredging to the deep cutting at Salwarpe; 1970s. (M. Sinclair)

same time as the Wednesbury Old Canal in the Black Country. All of a sudden, navvies were much in demand, and it wasn't long before those on the Droitwich were complaining about working conditions. Charles Hadfield in *Canals of the West Midlands*, provides an interesting little report, by the bricklayers engaged on the Droitwich: 'We af bin yoused very ill for thy will not pay for Wat we work for. If you don't pay for watt Time as bind we will not Work and wee will not work under 11 shillings a wick and to be yusde well.'

I wrongly assumed that the bricklayers then went back to work, but according to Max Sinclair, they were sacked, and then fined 5s; so much have the labour laws altered – for the better – over the years. Other bricklayers must have then been employed, for the Barge Canal was completed by March 1771. The people of Droitwich celebrated their good fortune. And then, nearly fifty years later, the Birmingham to Worcester Canal came past Droitwich in 1815, less than 2 miles to the east. The obvious step was to link the Barge Canal with the W&B, but this didn't happen for nearly forty years. Meanwhile, goods were being carried by land to Hanbury wharf to be transhipped onto narrowboats. When the short Junction Canal, as it was called, came into being in 1854, it was made with narrow locks, and the two waterways joined at the centre of Droitwich. Both canals were well utilised until about 1900, when there followed a steady decline until their final abandonment in 1939.

A PERSONAL VISIT IN 2008

Back in the summer of 2008, work on the Droitwich was progressing at a pace, and I was lucky to be invited along by Jason Leach, then British Waterways Manager of the whole project, to see what was going on and make a report to the canal press. Much good work had already been done to various sections of

The Raven Hotel, Droitwich and statue of a salt worker.

the canal, regarding dredging and towpath work. But at that very moment at locks four to six just north of the M5 motorway, many acres of land had been churned up by Morrison's massive earthmovers; while men in bright hardhats bobbed purposefully around the site. At the locks, hundreds of steel fixing rods pointed skyward out of bare concrete, and the site looked like a disaster zone. Plus at the time, two very serious problems needed to be solved. The canal had to be taken under the M5 Motorway embankment, and the even more massive bulk of the neighbouring A449.

I met Jason, went through a small Health and Safety induction, donned a hardhat and steel-capped wellies, and we ventured out onto the site for a tour. This particular section of the canal around locks four to six had been built over following the abandonment years, including a line of bungalows. That had given the designers a headache, and it required them to take a slightly different line from the original. As I looked at the area it was hard to imagine that order could come from such chaos. But Jason assured me that it would.

As we walked around the site it was interesting to contrast the modern way of making canals with the old way. Obviously technology plays a part, as does the introduction of new materials. We came across a number of concrete tubes. When I inquired what they were for, the answer was animal tunnels. Catering for the needs of small mammals was never in Brindley's or Priddey's list of requirements, but in today's modern world caring for the environment is an important part of canal planning. In the old days, Brindley would have probably done his survey

Information board at the Coney Meadow reed bed.

One of the streets of Droitwich with its charming medieval flavour.

on horseback; popping a wooden stake in here and there to mark the route. Then there would be a more careful setting of the levels with tripod and primitive theodolite (essentially a telescope with cross hairs). Today, Ground Positioning satellites are the means for setting things out, while laser beams set the levels. Bricks were extensively used in the early construction of locks and bridges; the search for suitable clay deposits along with the building of brick kilns was one of the first things to be accomplished. Today, the fixing of an inner steel framework and the erection of formwork provides the strength and mould for the pouring of ready-mixed concrete. Oh, and machines now put the puddling clay into place at the bed of the canal, and not the tramping feet of many navvies or even cow as was sometimes the case.

LOOKING AT OTHER AREAS

Some of the canal was in water in 2008, and the owner of the lock cottage at Ladywood had been running short boat trips for some time, as had the Droitwich Canal Trust (DCT). However, on inspection, there were several miles where the canal was completely choked with weed. That needed to be cleared and seriously dredged before any boats could pass along. The Barge Canal was not be dredged to its original dimensions, as only narrowboats would be catered for. All of the locks required much work, some, like the one at Hawford where the canal meets the River Severn, had almost disappeared, but the big engineering works as mentioned

Approaching the tunnel under the A449. It is worth making the point that the A449 at this location is as wide as any motorway, and was a huge obstacle to overcome. Notice that the canal is totally choked with reeds and other vegetation.

earlier were where the canal needed to go under the M5 Motorway and the A449. Those main arteries (the M5 in 1970) came long after the canal was abandoned, and it is fascinating now when you walk or cruise the canal to see how the civil engineers overcame those particular problems; so don't forget to admire them!

On the southern section of the canal, several miles were completely choked with weed. That has all now been cleared, and serious dredging has provided enough depth for the passing boats. The Barge Canal, however, was never going to be restored to its original dimensions as that would have been very costly, as well as being a waste of effort. Every single lock required work, some more than others, but especially the one where the canal meets the River Severn; that had almost disappeared into the undergrowth.

THE WRG GROUPS AND VOLUNTEERS

The freely given work of the Waterway Recovery Groups (WRG) and other volunteers was an essential part of the restoration, and I take my hardhat off to them. I went to see them at work in Vines Park in the centre of Droitwich on the same day. Chris Blaxland was in charge of the group, and they were tackling work on the first barge lock. This is the point where the River Salwarpe arrives in town, and a short section of this small river has been used in the navigation. The barge lock has, like all the other locks, deteriorated considerably, and Chris and his team were hard at work repairing brickwork and fitting the lock ladder that is now a necessary part of legislation. What continually impresses me is the fact that many people, young and old, sacrifice a week or more of their time to don Wellingtons

The point where the Barge Canal meets the Severn at Hawford Lock, 2008, with a weed-choked and derelict lock.

and hardhat and get their hands dirty. The WRGs perform skilled and non-skilled jobs, it depends on how much training each person has done. There were a couple of young ladies in the group, and I asked them how they came to be there. Their story is pretty typical of other young people who join the parties. They had been to college and university, but they wanted to get away from the academic world, and actually do something practical, to have the satisfaction of seeing what they had achieved. Others had been introduced into the WRG community by relatives. Others may have been involved with the Duke of Edinburgh Award. Whatever the reason, they all enjoy Britain's waterways, and get a great deal of pleasure from being engaged in a worthwhile project.

RESTORATION

Fast forward to July 2011, and the Barge Canal saw its first through traffic since 1919, when four private narrowboats, seven hire boats and two cruisers entered the river lock at Hawford. They made their historic journey along the delightfully wandering waterway with its eight restored locks to the town's old, yet new, canal basin at Netherwich. When I approached that very same basin on Sunday, 3 July, I was pleasantly confronted with a mass of colourful boats and lines of bunting. Visitors thronged the neighbouring park and towpath, while boaters happily sunned themselves on the back of their moored boats.

Speeches by officials were a programmed part of the weekend, and they lined up to offer congratulatory remarks and they couldn't praise the work of both volunteers and professionals enough; which is just about right. Environment

The same view three years later, with boats working the lock into the river.

Secretary Caroline Spellman MP kicked things off by unveiling the official plaque embedded in Vines Park, to record the illustrious event. She then spoke of her tribute to all those that had been involved in the forty-year restoration saying:

> Reconnecting and reopening the two canals is a great engineering achievement. I am delighted by the environmental sensitivity of the work. The new Coney Meadow reed bed is a marvellous example of ecological offsetting. This shows what can be achieved when local communities and national bodies come together and share responsibility for the waterways. Partnership of this sort shows that the future of the waterways in the charitable sector will be bright.

Tony Hales, chairman of what was then known as the British Waterways said:

> As a resident of Droitwich, when the Droitwich Canals Trust was formed, it was a wonderful day. A day that recognised vision, determination, skill, great patience and the real partnership between the local community, local and regional government and major national organisations. As British Waterways moves to a charity, this is exactly the sort of model we want going forward, when the national skills and resources of our team work hand in hand with our stakeholders, in particular local communities, as has been the case here, to deliver something for which we all share responsibility and ownership into the future.

Councillor Paul Middlebrough was next, remarking on the benefits to Droitwich. Vaughan Welch of the Droitwich Canals Trust (DCT) also praised the volunteers, as did Roger Hanbury, Chief Executive of the Canals Trust. And there were other kinds of celebrities. Historic British Waterways boats *Atlas* and *Malus* were amongst the first craft to take a test run of the restored waterways prior to the opening weekend, and they looked fabulous in the sunshine when moored up in Vines Park. Still it was a tight fit in places, with little more than an inch of headroom to spare in the culverted tunnel under the M5, and some grounding in mud for the deep draughted *Atlas*; something that will be addressed by dredging teams. Following the blue and yellow BW boats was IWA chairman Clive Henderson in his boat *Nanshe*. He said that he was deeply honoured to be on the first leisure boat to make the full passage

As I mentioned earlier, thousands of people have been involved in the £12 million, forty-year enterprise to restore the Droitwich canals, from world class engineers and councillors, to litter pickers. But someone who should get a mention is Max Sinclair. Max was there right from the beginning, back in those distant 1960s and early 1970s, and, thankfully, he was present for the opening weekend. As president of the DCT he said that it was an emotional day for him, as he had been dreaming of that very special moment for fifty years, ever since he and his wife Jocelyn joined the Inland Waterways Association (IWA) back in 1959. They, along with others, made tiny steps during the early years, but never wavered in their campaigning once started. But when he saw the first-class moorings near Vine Park, he said that it was hard to remember the time when the first half-mile of the canal outside town had been covered by a sewage

Ladywood Lock Cottage being rebuilt sometime during the 1970s. (M. Sinclair)

works. The reeds were supposedly 'Dutch style' to purify the water; unfortunately poisonous chemicals from the towns industries meant that it hadn't worked.

The way that people get motivated to a particular task or project is a fascinating subject, but Max remembers how it started for him. Like so many waterways restorers, he was inspired by the leadership of the pioneering David Hutchings and his work on the Stratford Canal. He realised that what was happening on the Stratford was possible at Droitwich. Guided by David, and encouraged by local IWA chairman Michael McFarlane, Max started correspondence with local councils and newspapers, proposing restoration for the benefit of the local community. This only brought a mass of opposition from farmers, landowners, householders and councillors. Many had been quietly encroaching on canal land, and fiercely resisted restoration.

Later they began to receive support from the town architect, though there were opposing factions within the council, and even sabotage. The canal was filled in with thousands of tons of spoil from the making of the M5, while a bowling green was built across the line of the canal. These bad decisions would cost the council dearly in the years ahead. But on the 12 March 1971, exactly 200 years to the day from the canal's opening, the very first work party was organised by members of the Worcester and Birmingham Canal Society, and they began to unearth the canal. Then later, in 1973, a massive work party was organised, this time by the new Droitwich Canals Trust, when nearly 1,000 people turned up to attack the thick undergrowth. Good press coverage ensued – always a necessary help, and needed funds were raised. The Trust was then given a ninety-year lease for restoration, and the ball was rolling.

Netherwich Basin near Vines Park being pumped out. (M. Sinclair)

Clearing Porters Mill Lock (No.4), with Chris Burton raising a shovel. (M. Sinclair)

Down at Ladywood, a full-time manager was installed at the tumbledown cottage, where the DCT set up its lock gate workshops. One of the first to join was Dick Pearson, who started a successful lock restoration programme. He in turn was followed by Dave and Izzy Turner, who constructed a mile of narrow gauge railway to spread 300,000 tons of soil from the canal into the local fields. Work carried on with assistance from WRG parties, the Royal engineers and many others who were simply enthused by the whole project.

It was only when Max carried out more research that he came to realise that the Droitwich, small as it was, was a major part of waterways history. The original engineer, James Brindley, described Hawford Lock – where the Barge Canal joins the Severn – as a work that he was most proud of. Certainly building and keeping dry lime mortar brickwork must have been a difficult task, with wooden pumps working around the clock. In those days, builders had little confidence in structural brickwork, as the bricks were fired at low temperatures in the temporary kilns erected close to the construction sites. Nevertheless, that primitive technology, with each lock built with elm wall plates and mortised and tenoned frames, has survived admirably, preserved by the high salt content of the water.

During a marvellous three-day trip of the canal and its neighbours, Max said that it was an emotional experience, full of fine memories of the many volunteers that had sacrificed their time and contributed much to the restoration. As he watched the boats in the restored Netherwich Basin, Max was filled with pride and satisfaction at the magnificent waterway. Visiting boaters were heard to remark 'What a lovely canal' which was very pleasing to hear. Max had glowing praise for Jason Leach, the senior engineer, who drove the restoration to its triumphant

Vines Park during the opening celebrations 2011, with historic British Waterways boats, *Atlas* and *Malus*.

The opening celebratory weekend at Vines Park, Droitwich, 3 July 2011.

conclusion in July 2011. 'He was wonderful,' said Max. 'He's brought all the partners together, and fought his corner to keep the project going whenever there was disagreement. It couldn't have happened so quickly without him.'

Jason was also magnanimous with his remarks, stating that it was, 'rewarding to see all the diverse efforts of groups and individuals coming to fruition after decades of planning and spadework.' He continued, 'The £12 million project to restore those canals would prove to be an economic generator, a green corridor for communities and a magnet for visiting boaters. Certainly all involved, especially the Droitwich Canals Trust for their unstinting perseverance in the early days, deserve the highest praise. And, I am convinced that this superb, wonderful new route will prove to be increasingly popular and much loved as the years go by.'

MAX'S NOTES ON THE DEMISE OF THE ONCE AND GLORIOUS SALT TRADE; AND FINAL TRAFFIC ON EITHER CANAL

In the early 1900s all the salt manufacturers were highly dependent on a single customer, The British Alkali Company, of Bristol, who consumed a considerable tonnage of salt delivered by boat and rail. This was used for production of sulphuric acid in vast quantities for the armaments industry supplying the First World War. In 1916, a telegram was received at the Salt Union office cancelling all orders and refusing any more deliveries. Droitwich barges in Bristol, two on the Severn and three on the canal, were ordered to return to the town.

ICI Ltd at Nantwich and Stoke Bromsgrove had adopted the patented Mond process of boiling brine in a vacuum, which used considerably less coal to evaporate and was considerably cheaper. This was a great shock to the town and rapidly a delegation comprising the local MP, Mayor, councillors, and Salt Union directors travelled to Bristol to try and negotiate a reinstatement, but without success.

It's not difficult to imagine what a miserable business it must have been for the owner/skippers and their mates to have to shovel and wheelbarrow 90 tons of salt back into the already loaded warehouses. They must have known there would

Approaching the barge lock on the canal, with the River Salwarpe just in front of the houses.

be no future demand for their services. From then on only a small quantity of salt was supplied for domestic purposes. This was most unfortunate as Droitwich salt deposits are totally pure, without any bitter sand content. Housewives, including my grandmother, used it annually to salt eggs, runner and broad beans in large glass jars for the kitchen's winter supply.

The barge fleet was dismasted and towed to Gloucester for use in the busy docks as dumb lighters. The owners must have received only a fraction of their value.

The last cargo on the Barge Canal was by *Volunteer*, which loaded two hayricks commandeered at Mildenham Mill by army officers to feed horses in France, where over two million required supplies. On board, as it was bow hauled down the canal, was 'Lol' Brown, a fourteen year old who was going into the Navy. The miller, Bill Watts, referred to it as theft at gunpoint. Lol told me the haulers chanted a shanty with the crew replying, surely the last time a sea shanty was heard in the Midlands. In a chain of boats they went to Cardiff Docks where, by coincidence, my mother worked in the office at the East Dock registering supplies. She was a stenographer working for Mr Kay at Kay's, but along with other girls was conscripted for this vital war work. They slept in the warehouse with the rats. The Droitwich barges had white sails; the East Coast practise of dressing the sailcloth to preserve it with a foul-smelling concoction of fish oil and red lead powder was not adopted on the Severn.

Cruising through the new locks on the Junction Canal, July 2011. A magnificent achievement.

Max Sinclair, born in 1930 at the opening ceremony, with Jason Leach, in 2011.

The last surviving working Droitwich boat was the *Rose*, which ended her life sailing the lower Severn Estuary placing large rocks to reinforce the banks until she was broken up just downstream of Lydney harbour. So died this remarkable fleet whose skippers kissed their wives goodbye in Droitwich and faced the challenges of the Bristol Channel, Welsh coast, English Channel and French coast supplying the fishing ports until refrigeration was invented.

On the Junction Canal the only traffic after 1916 was a weekly horse-drawn narrowboat laden with town rubbish to discharge into the Hanbury Brickworks clay pit, sometimes returning with bricks. No motor boats are recorded working through Droitwich as they were not devised before the trade ceased.

There was a steam pleasure boat, *The Coronation*, giving local trips and housed in the Hampton Road boathouse before the war and now used by the Boxing Club. A lovely Worcester Birmingham tug *The Lady Harriet* occasionally passed through the canals heading for Bevere. And finally, a small fleet of rowing boats could be hired at weekends for pleasure seekers to row to Ladywood for tea.

If you enjoyed this book, you may also be interested in...

Midlands Canals

ROBERT DAVIES

Compiles interviews with boat people and the people who worked th
inland waterways during the final decades of commercial canal carrying
This book spans the 1930s–'60s, a time when transport technology sav
changes, and looks issues such as the operating of ice boats and the use c
horse power as well as the experiences of the people themselves.

978 0 7524 3910 5

Great War Britain Birmingham: Remembering 1914-18

SIAN ROBERTS

The First World War claimed over 900,000 British lives, and its legacy
continues to be remembered today. Great War Britain: Birmingham
offers an in-depth portrait of the county and its people during the
'war to end all wars'. Vividly illustrated with evocative images, it
commemorates the bravery and sacrifice of Birmingham's people
between 1914 and 1918

978 0 7509 5969 8

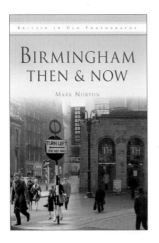

Birmingham Then & Now

MARK NORTON

Take a fascinating and nostalgic visual journey back to 1960s
Birmingham to witness the much-loved Bull Ring, the grand city-
centre buildings that were demolished to make way for the 'modern'
city and the streets and courts that were swept away during the last fifty
years of development.

978 0 7524 5722 2

Visit our website and discover thousands of other History Press books.

www.thehistorypress.co.uk